CLASSIC
AFTER-DINNER
SPORTS TALES

CLASSIC
AFTER-DINNER
SPORTS TALES

Compiled by
Jonathan Rice

CollinsWillow
An Imprint of HarperCollinsPublishers

First published in Great Britain in 2004 by CollinsWillow
an imprint of HarperCollins*Publishers* London

This paperback edition first published in 2005
by HarperCollins*Publishers*

Text copyright © Compilation 2004 Jonathan Rice
Illustrations courtesy of Bill Tidy

1

A CIP catalogue record for this book
is available from the British Library

The HarperCollins website address is:
www.harpercollins.co.uk/entertainment

ISBN 0 00 718990 7

Printed and bound in Great Britain by
Clays Ltd, St Ives Plc

Picture acknowledgements
Page 1 top © Corbis; middle © David Jacobs/Action Images: **Page 2** top
© Michael Regan/Action Images; bottom © Alex Morton/Action Images:
Page 3 © Otto Greule Jr/Getty Images: **Page 4** top © Ker Robertson/
Getty Images; middle © Jason O'Brien/Action Images; bottom © Steve
Mitchell/Empics: **Page 5** top © Clive Brunskill/Getty Images; middle
© David Rogers/Getty Images; bottom © Wally McNamee/Corbis: **Page 6**
top © Neil Tingle/Action Plus; bottom © Glyn Kirk/Action Plus: **Page 7**
top © Tony Marshall/Empics; bottom © John Gichigi/Getty Images:
Page 8 top © Neil Tingle/Action Plus; middle © Michael Regan/Action
Images: **Page 9** © Alex Morton/Action Images: **Page 10** top © Julian
Herbert/Getty Images; bottom © John Gichigi/Getty Images: **Page 11**
top © Mark Thompson/Getty Images; bottom © Chris McGrath/Getty
Images: **Page 12** top © Darren Walsh/Action Images; middle © Chris
Trotman/Corbis; bottom © Glyn Kirk/Action Plus: **Page 13** © Corbis:
Page 14 top © Tony Marshall/Empics; middle © Jean-Paul Pelissier/Corbis;
bottom © Mike Egerton/Empics: **Page 15** top © Glyn Kirk/Action Plus;
bottom © P. Lahalle/Corbis: **Page 16** top © Glyn Kirk/Action Plus; middle
© John Sibley/Action Images.

ACKNOWLEDGEMENTS

———◄◇►———

Putting together this book has been a team effort. There are many people who have to be thanked, not least the contributors. Many of them came up with original stories after only being asked once, and even those we had to chase until they felt like cornered foxes came up with the goods graciously and to great effect.

Getting to all these stars is quite a trick. Without The Lord's Taverners address book, so ably wielded by Derrin Gill, we would have been about 150 stories short of a book. Mark Williams, Chief Executive of The Lord's Taverners, has also come up with a number of key contacts which proved very useful. I must also acknowledge the tremendous help given by Tim Scott, whose contacts in South Africa came up trumps, along with David Gemmell and my brothers Andy and Tim Rice, not to mention my son Alex Rice at BBC Radio Five Live, who between them have access to all sorts of people in all parts of the globe. Graeme Wright, Ian Wooldridge and Bill Russell also introduced me to a number of important names, for which many thanks.

Thanks are also due to Pam Ayres and Weidenfeld & Nicolson for permission to reproduce her poem, 'How Can That Be My Baby?'; to Max Boyce for allowing us to use his stories; and to Bob 'The Cat' Bevan and Virgin Books for permission to adapt a couple of stories from his autobiography, *Nearly Famous*. All other stories, to the best of our knowledge, have not been published elsewhere before.

Bill Tidy's cartoons are as brilliant as ever, and as quickly produced and as gladly provided as ever, which helps! Thanks also to Geoffrey Chater for providing the photograph of the 1953 Lord's Taverners XI. At HarperCollins, Michael Doggart and Tarda Davison-Aitkins have been encouraging and helpful while I have slowly compiled the list of runners and riders (and cricketers and footballers and rugby players and sailors and boxers and so on).

To all, and to everyone, thanks.

Jonathan Rice
May 2004

INTRODUCTION

By Mike Gatting
President of The Lord's Taverners

Becoming well known as a sportsman has many advantages. When you play well, or your team wins something, people will stop you in the street to say, 'Well done', or give you the thumbs up or their half of a high five as they drive by. Sometimes their appreciation will be more practical, as with the Northamptonshire butcher who gave David Steele a lamb chop (or was it pork?) for every one of the 365 Test runs he scored against the Australians in 1975. Nobody ever offered me anything as good as that.

And then there's the hero worship. I'm not saying that sportsmen are worthy of the treatment we get from the fans, but not many people outside films or rock and roll get to have their photos stuck up on teenage bedroom walls, especially with my basic shape and looks. All the same, it's great to know that there's a whole lot of people out there who have put their faith in you, and believe you can score those runs, that goal, that try or hole that putt. It makes you believe that little bit more in yourself.

But there is, inevitably, a downside to fame. Everybody who becomes a 'personality' seems to be expected to give speeches at business gatherings, at supermarket openings or, most frequently, after dinners where, as the late Willie Rushton used to say, it was an achievement to be able to stand up, let alone speak. Politicians and actors have the advantage over sportsmen here, because speaking is their livelihood: that's how they make their money. But for sportsmen and women, it can be much more frightening. After all, the most we speak in public while we are actually earning our living is to shout, 'Howzat!' or 'Oi, ref!', which is not too difficult to learn to say without forgetting the words or dropping the sheet of paper they were written on.

Some people are good at speaking in public – people like Richie Benaud, Henry Cooper, Fred Trueman and JPR Williams, all of whom feature in this book – but most of us have to learn the hard way. We've all had the experience of telling the wrong joke to the wrong audience, or of having to follow another speaker who has turned out to be so good that there is no chance that any of the diners will want to listen to our feeble effort – assuming that is, they haven't got up to go to the loo at the end of his speech.

Fortunately, sport is a rich goldmine of funny stories and almost everybody has got at least one to tell. Many of them have found their way into this book. I suppose it's because sportsmen and women at the top of their sports are so very good at what they do that any failure, any lapse in the perfection of their play, gives those who could never hope to be that good a chance to realise that even a Muhammad Ali, a Garry Sobers or a Bobby Charlton is still a human being. And it helps if you can laugh at yourself, whatever you do in life. A sense of humour is probably more important in sport than in most other professions. The life can be so unreal sometimes that we all need a way of keeping our feet on the ground.

This book has been put together in aid of The Lord's Taverners, the charity that is also a club, whose aim is 'to give young people, particularly those with special needs, a

The Lord's Taverners XI against Bishop's Stortford in August 1953, including Denis Compton and Godfrey Evans.

sporting chance'. We raise money in all sorts of ways and for various causes: to provide funds for youth cricket; to purchase minibuses to provide transportation to recreational and sporting activities for disabled young people; to provide sports wheelchairs for young people; and to finance specialised equipment for young people with special needs. Events are held all around the country throughout the year, raising about £2 million each year to help young people have greater access to sport.

The charity has been in existence since 1950, when it was formed by a group of actors who used to enjoy the cricket from outside the old Lord's Tavern, and thought it would be good to give something back to the game that had given them so much pleasure. You will see from the list of contributors how close the links are between cricket and acting: there's Donald Sinden, William Franklyn, Burt Kwouk, Wendy Richard and June Whitfield to name but some, and our first President, Sir John Mills, is still involved with the charity. It is a huge thrill to be the President in 2004, following in such exalted footsteps.

I hope you enjoy this book. We very much appreciate the time and trouble a whole lot of well-known and busy people took to help us put it together. And next time I have to stand up to speak to a crowd of eager or inebriated people, I will have a whole hoard of new stories to make use of.

Mike Gatting
2004

CONTRIBUTORS

A
David ACFIELD
Chris ADAMS
Kay ALEXANDER
Dennis AMISS
Rodger ARNEIL
Michael ASPEL
Pam AYRES

B
Trevor BAILEY
John BARCLAY
Eddie BARLOW
Alec BEDSER
Derek BELL
Richie BENAUD
Bob 'The Cat' BEVAN
Harold 'Dickie' BIRD
Naas BOTHA
Ian BOTHAM
Max BOYCE

C
Geoffrey CHATER
Ray CONNOLLY
Henry COOPER
Bob COTTAM
Stephen COVERDALE
Chris COWDREY
John CRAWLEY
Robert CROFT
Barry CRYER

D
Dickie DAVIES
Gareth Y DAVIES
Kevin DEVINE
Pat DEWES
Jason DODD
Neil DURDEN SMITH

E
Jane EAGLEN
Rod EDDINGTON

11

Frances EDMONDS
Bella EMBERG

F

Theo FENNELL
Keith FLETCHER
Dick FRANCIS
William FRANKLYN
Angus FRASER
Liz FRASER

G

Paul GAMBACCINI
Lesley GARRETT
Mike GATTING
David GEMMELL
Calum GILES
Ian GILLAN
Evelyn GLENNIE
Graham GOOCH
Charmian GRADWELL
Tanni GREY THOMPSON
Sheila GRIER

H

Jeremy HANLEY
Tanya HARFORD
Miles HARRISON
Howard HASLETT
Scott HASTINGS
Tim HEALD
Jimmy HILL
Richard HILLS
Frazer HINES

Liz HOBBS
Roy HUDD
Andrew HUDSON
Simon HUGHES
Jenny HULL

I

Colin INGLEBY-MACKENZIE

J

Anthony JEFFERSON
Charles JEFFREY
John JEFFREY
David JENSEN
Graham JOHNSON
Sally JONES
Steve JONES

K

Richard KERR
Richard KERSHAW
John KETTLEY
Roger KNIGHT
Alan KNOTT
Burt KWOUK

L

Renton LAIDLAW
Tim LAMB
George LAYTON
Gary LINEKER
Julian LLOYD WEBBER

M

Martin McCAGUE
Liz McCOLGAN
Ian McINTOSH
Mick McMANUS
Christopher MARTIN-
    JENKINS
Christopher MATTHEW
Michael MELLUISH
June MENDOZA
Murray MEXTED
Vicki MICHELLE
Adrian MILLS
Hector MONRO
Patrick MOORE
Diana MORAN
Joan MORECAMBE
Martyn MOXON
Al MURRAY

N

Don NEELY
Gary NEWBON
Paul NIXON

O

Nick OWEN

P

Cecil PARKINSON
Nicholas PARSONS
Min PATEL
Mary PETERS
Gene PITNEY

Peter POLYCARPOU
Robert POWELL
Kieran PRENDIVILLE
David PURDIE

Q

Trevor QUIRK

R

Clive RADLEY
Chris REA
Jonty RHODES
Tim RICE
Wendy RICHARD
David RIPLEY
John ROBBIE
Tim ROBINSON
Bobby ROBSON
Struan RODGER
Budge ROGERS
Adrian ROLLINS
Joseph ROMANOS
Graham ROSE
Gerallt ROSSER
Rob ROTH

S

Brough SCOTT
David SHEEPSHANKS
David SHEPPARD
Ned SHERRIN
Dennis SILK
Alan SIMPSON
Reg SIMPSON

Donald SINDEN
Keith SMITH
Mike SMITH
Francis STAFFORD
John STAPLETON
Sheila STEAFEL
David STEELE
Andy STEGGALL
Richard STILGOE

T
Chris TARRANT
Chris TAVARE
Shaw TAYLOR
Stan TAYLOR
Robert TEAR
Gary TEICHMANN
Leslie THOMAS
Bill THRELFALL
Bill TIDY
Alan TITCHMARSH
Sam TORRANCE
Tim TREMLETT
Fred TRUEMAN

Christine TRUMAN JANES
Stuart TURNER
Julian TUTT

V
Peter VAUGHAN
Debra VEAL
Brian VINER

W
Graham WALKER
John WARNETT
Steve WATKIN
Vince WELLS
Mike WESTON
Richard WHITELEY
June WHITFIELD
JPR WILLIAMS
Shaun WILLIAMSON
Julian WILSON
Andrew WINGFIELD DIGBY
Greg WISE
John WOODCOCK
Ian WOOLDRIDGE

A

DAVID ACFIELD

◄◇►

*Former Cambridge University and Essex off-spinner,
and international fencer, who competed in the 1968
and 1972 Olympic Games for Great Britain. Later a
member of ECB's cricket committee.*

I played in an Essex side renowned for its sense of humour –
for example, Keith Pont at Burton, having run from third
man to fine leg every over for much of the day, was
seen riding a bicycle across the outfield to get to his position
– probably a unique event in first class cricket.

My batting was not my strength. I was never at my
best against West Indian quicks, and as we were leading
Hampshire in a county game by 200 or so, the second new
ball was due and I was next in, I suggested to our captain
Keith Fletcher that it would be an appropriate time to
declare.

His considered reply was that it would be a shame to
deprive the crowd (and him) of the spectacle of me facing
Malcolm Marshall armed with a new ball. As I sat there, all

padded up and trembling, he helped my resolve with such comments as,' He won't get you out straight away, he'll chip bits off you first!'

When I reached the wicket I informed Brian Hardie, who had already scored a century, that I wasn't coming down that end – this ball, next ball or any other **** ball' – and I never did, despite the Hampshire captain putting all the fielders on the boundary. When the ball was rolled in I fetched it and handed it politely to Mr. Marshall until our captain decided that the farce had lasted long enough. Another proud not out.

My batting was best summed up by John Reason in *The Daily Telegraph* when he wrote of my innings for Cambridge University v West Indies thus:

'Acfield rocked to his forward prod and back again irrespective of contact. Mostly he deposited the ball politely in front of the fielders and once he hit the ball hard enough to say, "Wait".'

CHRIS ADAMS

—◇—

*Derbyshire, Sussex and England batsman
who led Sussex to their first ever County
Championship title in 2003. A Wisden
Cricketer of the Year in 2004.*

In the rain-affected Fifth Test against South Africa at Centurion Park in January 2000, our physio Dean Conway suggested to the England team that a session of weights in the gym might alleviate the boredom of watching the rain.

Darren Gough's response was, 'I don't need no weights.'

Flexing his torso he then said, 'You know why they call me Rhino at Yorkshire, don't you? Because I'm as strong as an ox'!

KAY ALEXANDER

BBC television news presenter, based in the Midlands.

Beginner's Rugby

Surly 11-year-old: 'I don't want to play rugby!'

Harrassed mother: 'Why don't you? It was your grandfather's favourite game, it's your father's favourite game, it's a fantastic game, why don't you want to play it?'

Surly 11-year-old: 'Well how would you like it, standing around in the freezing-cold for hours doing nothing, then when you do do something, you get mugged!'

DENNIS AMISS

Warwickshire and England opening batsman, who played fifty Tests for England in the 1970s, scoring 3,612 runs at an average of 46.30. Subsequently became Warwickshire's Chief Executive.

We were in Antigua during MCC's tour of West Indies in early 1974. Next to the cricket ground was Antigua's prison. Mike Denness, our captain, saw two chaps rolling the wicket on the morning of the match, and went over to speak to them.

'How long have you been rolling the wicket for?' he asked.

Back came the reply, 'Twenty-five years, boss.' They were both serving life sentences in the prison across the road.

RODGER ARNEIL

<><o><>

Former Scottish flanker and captain. He toured with the British Lions in 1968 and 1971.

In 1969 I was picked to play for Scotland against France at Stade Colombes in Paris. We had a memorable weekend in the hands of the Scottish Rugby Union.

At that time the members of the Scotland Rugby Team were allowed one international jersey for the season and had to bring along a pair of clean white shorts and navy blue stockings for the game. If match jerseys were swapped with the opposition the player was then invoiced for a replacement jersey for the next match. Luckily my travel costs for the season offset my jersey costs so I broke even. The SRU fervently believed in the amateur status and implemented their beliefs to the letter.

On the Wednesday before the game I received an international telephone call at my home in Scotland from a representative of a famous German sports equipment manufacturer. The soothing and polished voice on the telephone, after the exchange of the usual courtesies, asked me if I would like to try out a pair of their super new boots for the game.

As I was broke and my boots were falling apart I replied slowly, trying to play hard to get. I did not give an immediate 'yeees' but hesitated, saying that I was not really sure but if he could manage two pairs I would consider trying them out.

'No problem,' he said. 'I shall deliver them to your hotel in Paris.'

The next day the team left Edinburgh on a charter flight with the usual contingent of alickadoos and their wives all out for a wonderful expenses-paid weekend. The gin and tonics flowed as soon as the plane lifted off and we were on our way to Paris. I sat with the team in the rear seats dreaming of my new boots. I had told no one of the arrangement.

On arrival in Paris we made our way to the hotel in the team bus and checked in. I put the key in the lock and opened the door of my room. The far wall of the room was stacked with boxes of at least 60 pairs of gleaming new rugby boots.

The smooth German promotions manager appeared from nowhere asking if the rest of the lads would like a pair. Nairn McEwen my room-mate looked perplexed, fearful of the consequences. It was his first international for Scotland. The other players passing in the corridor could not help but notice the boxes of boots and soon the whole team knew.

We held an emergency meeting. Ian Robertson of BBC fame and Mike Smith the Cambridge wing, both considered two of the more intelligent members of the team, proclaimed that we should tell the manager. They reasoned that depending on the degree of alcohol consumed there was a possibility that he might notice that the team would all have polished new boots with three stripes on them next day for the game instead of the dirty old boots that was the usual turnout.

The manager was called and considered the situation with gravity. He huffed and puffed about professionalism and what the committee would think. He was swiftly given another gin and tonic and asked if he would like to try on a pair. His mood changed and he began to smile as he admired the way the shiny new boots fitted him perfectly.

Without further ado he gave the order – charge everyone who wants a pair 50p and that'll be the end of it. With that he put the new boots under his arm and walked off down the corridor to join the rest of the committee for another gin and tonic, announcing his decision and showing off his new acquisitions.

Eventually all the committee and even some of the wives had a pair!

Nairn was aghast and was in shock, saying that he needed a bath to relax. After the bath it was time for bed and he asked me what I thought about Benoit Dauga, the French no. 8.

Nairn was about 5ft 6" and 12 stones, Benoit was around 6ft 8" and 16 stones of muscle. 'Is he dirty? Is he fast?' Nairn asked with concern in his eyes. I replied that Benoit was the fastest nastiest player ever to grace a rugby field. Nairn went quiet.

In the morning I asked Nairn how he had slept. He said he hadn't slept a wink and had worried and sweated all through the night.

Scotland won the match beating France 9–3. We all wore our new boots, which were shown on television, and Nairn played like a man possessed. The three stripes became a marque of the sport and the SRU committee changed forever from the amateur to professional status. It was a benchmark in the annals of Scottish rugby football history and things have never been the same since.

"..PLUS £1-14-6½d OF MURRAYFIELD MUD ON THE SWAPPED JERSEY..."

MICHAEL ASPEL

*Television broadcaster whose career has included
BBC television newscasting,* Crackerjack, This
Is Your Life *and* The Antiques Roadshow,
among many other credits.

One summer's day in the early 1980s, I was sitting at a lake-side café in Italy (to be precise, it was Orta San Giulio, later featured annoyingly by Judith Chalmers in her list of great places to visit – thus spoiling it for us regulars).

As I sipped my Prosecco, I noticed a commotion in the water about one hundred yards out. Someone was trying to water-ski, and was failing spectacularly. After many attempts, he finally rose from the water and managed to stay upright for a few seconds. Then one ski flew off at an angle and the other one disappeared; by the laws of gravity the skier should have done the same. But he was so desperate to keep going that he held on to the tow rope and actually ran across the surface of the lake for about six paces.

When I eventually stopped laughing, I decided it was time to resurrect my own watersports career. So that afternoon, I went out with the hotel boat, and although it had been a few years since I'd last been on skis, I got up at once and in a few seconds was flying along. I had told the crew my intention was to do a bit of mono-skiing, so I transferred my weight to the left, slipped off the right ski and really started to move. Halfway across the lake, I came off and hit the water at a tremendous speed.

Now, if you are going to do that, you should try to land face forward or on your back, or even on your elbows – but not on your backside. Not at speed, not into water. A gallon of Lake Orta entered me through orifices I didn't know I had.

Through the pain, words like 'enema', 'douche' and 'emasculation' drifted into my mind. I had visions of sitting down to dinner that night, and streams jetting from my ears.

Luckily, there was no real damage. I just had rather a strange walk for a few days, which my family seemed to find amusing. I don't think you should laugh at other people's suffering.

PAM AYRES

<o>

Very popular comedienne, poet and television personality who has been a keen member of the Lady Taverners for many years.

HOW CAN THAT BE MY BABY?
How can that be my baby? How can that be my son?
Standing on a rugger field, more than six feet one.

Steam is rising from him, his legs are streaked with blood,
And he wears a yellow mouthguard in a face that's black
    with mud.

How can that be my baby? How can he look like that?
I used to sit him on my knee and read him Postman Pat.
Those little ears with cotton buds I kept in perfect shape,
But now they're big and purple and fastened back with tape.

How can that be my baby? When did he reach that size?
What happened to his wellies with the little froggy eyes?
His shirt is on one shoulder but it's hanging off the other,
And the little baffled person at his feet is me: his mother.

B

TREVOR BAILEY

<o>

*One of English cricket's greatest all-rounders, he played
for Cambridge University, Essex and England between
1945 and 1967, playing 61 times for England. A true
all-rounder, he was also a very accomplished footballer
and subsequently a noted sports journalist.*

I loved playing cricket and became very involved in every
aspect, but once a county match, or a Test match, was over I
very quickly forgot the runs, the wickets, the catches, the
scores, the players and even the outcome. I just remembered
the incidents that appealed to me. For example, I shall
always treasure a few moments of magic at Chelmsford,
when Essex met Sussex in the early fifties. The visitors had
established a substantial lead and a declaration was imminent, when I happened to take a wicket with the fourth ball
of my over. This brought Robin Marlar, who had been
appointed captain of Sussex that year, to the crease. Before
taking guard, Robin summoned his partner, George Cox, to
the middle of the pitch for a discussion.

Eventually I was able to deliver my fifth ball, which happened to be straight and sent his middle stump for a walk, while at the same time the two batsmen were about to cross in the middle of the pitch, attempting to take a run to the keeper and give George the strike. The declaration was immediate and we all walked off the field with the entire Essex team in tears of laughter.

* * *

Another magic moment occurred in South Africa, when a quarter of an hour before the start of the First Test in Johannesburg in December 1956, Peter May asked me to open the innings with Peter Richardson. I immediately asked my partner if he realised that we were taking on the roles of high-class batsmen in English cricket history, like Hobbs and Sutcliffe, who had both possessed an ability and repertoire of strokes of an entirely different class to what we had to offer. The outcome was that we went out to the middle with Peter as Herbert Sutcliffe and myself as Sir John.

Our shouts of 'Get back, Sir John,' and 'Come one, Herbert' certainly surprised the opposition as I do not think that frivolity of this kind was quite their scene. However, it worked rather better than either Peter or I expected, as we made a good start and Peter went on to make a solid century.

JOHN BARCLAY

◄○►

Captain of Sussex from 1981 to 1986, he scored almost 10,000 runs, including 9 centuries, and took 324 wickets with his off-breaks. Subsequently a leading cricket administrator.

Middlesex v Sussex at Hove in 1980 – I toss up with Mike Brearley and win the toss. Walking back to the pavilion to convey this news to the team, I was addressed by a lady at the boundary edge.

'Mr. Barclay,' she said. 'Have you won the toss?'

'Yes,' I replied proudly.

'And are you going to bat?'

'Yes,' I said, even more proudly.

'And are you opening the batting?'

'Yes,' I said, puffing out my chest.

'In that case,' said the lady, 'I'll go into Hove to do my Sainsbury's shop before lunch.'

EDDIE BARLOW

―◄○►―

*One of the all-time great South African cricketers, Eddie
Barlow played 30 times for his country before South
Africa's exclusion in 1970. He scored 2,516 runs at an
average of 45.74, and took 40 wickets. He subsequently
played for Derbyshire with distinction.*

When I began my cricketing career, it started, like most boys,
in my parents' back garden. My brother Norman and I were
limited by space and had to share our ground with Dad's vegetable garden. He was very proud of his achievements and had
grown some wonderful cauliflowers. Unfortunately they were
right in the firing line of Norman's cover drives and sure
enough one of these knocked a top completely off, quickly followed by another one. With great presence of mind we sat the
tops back on their stalks and carried on playing. A few days
later we spotted Dad inspecting his handiwork, seeing his face
turn from pleasure to anger. Now we were going to catch it. As
he came inside we heard him say to Mum, 'Those wretched
cutworms have ruined my caulies.' Phew! Saved by the worms.

*   *   *

Whiling away the time in Australia we asked each other how
we had got our names. Mine, Barlow, I said came about
because a Mr Bar who owned a pub married a Miss Low who
was not very tall. Peter Carlstein, we said, was related to the
Swedish King Carl Gustav, hence the Carl, and his ancestor
had married a princess of Stein. Johnny Waite and I decided
to carry the game a little further and on the day of the first
Test he received a telegram, common in those days, which
said 'Good luck Peter from Gus'.

'Who the hell is Gus?' asked Peter. 'Well, obviously it

is the King of Sweden,' we said, and some good-natured ribbing ensued. The word must have got out for when he walked out to the crease and took guard, Wally Grout greeted him with the words. 'Good morning Your Royal Highness,' He was out first ball to Richie Benaud's famous flipper.

ALEC BEDSER

—◄○►—

Probably the greatest fast-medium bowler ever to have played for England, Sir Alec Bedser CBE carried the England bowling attack in the years immediately after World War II. By the time he retired, he had taken 236 Test wickets – a record at the time, including 39 in the Ashes-winning series of 1953.

In 1946, Surrey CCC played a match in aid of the club's Centenary Appeal Fund, against an Old England Eleven. Some 18,000 spectators came. The Old England side comprised Sutcliffe, Sandham, Hendren, Woolley, Jardine, Tate and M.J.C. Allom among others. The captain was Percy Fender. Surrey fielded their full county side but the match was obviously played in a light-hearted way.

Frank Woolley, the great Kent and England batsman, made a good score, and during his innings, my brother Eric and I decided to have a bit of fun. Frank Woolley had not met us, and did not know we were twins. Eric bowled slow off-spinners and I bowled fast-medium. We decided to bowl one over between us. I bowled the first three balls to Frank Woolley, and then we switched over in a way that nobody noticed, so that Eric bowled the last three balls. At the end of the over, Frank Woolley turned to our wicket-keeper and

said, 'That young man has a wonderful change of pace.'
Everybody had a good laugh, including Frank, when we
explained the trick to him.

DEREK BELL

◄○►

*Racing driver who competed at Formula 3, Formula 2
and Formula 1 before going on to become one of the
leading sports car drivers of his generation. He won two
World Sportscar titles (in 1985 and 1986), five victories
in the Le Mans 24 Hours and three in Daytona 24
Hours, between 1975 and 1987.*

The car that didn't make it.
   A well-respected racing driver was invited by the designer

to test a particularly poor-handling racing car. After a few laps at a modest pace at Silverstone, the driver pulled into the pits, climbed out of the car, removed his helmet, looked at the designer and, with his broad Aussie accent, said, 'John, you are a bloody genius!'

John was overcome with excitement that this star driver thought his car so good!

'Really Frank?' the designer said.

'Yes John, you have two cars here, one at the front and one at the back'... and he strolled off.

RICHIE BENAUD

Not only one of the great leg-spinners and captains in Australia's cricket history, a man who retired after taking 248 wickets and scoring 2,201 runs in his 63 Tests, but also one of the legendary cricket commentators, whose laconic and precise style is often imitated but rarely matched.

Some cricket spectators have long memories. A few are brilliant with their repartee and, when they marry that with a good memory, the effect can be devastating.

Forty-nine years ago, I toured the West Indies and played in all five Tests. This had come at the end of a rather harrowing experience in Australia against Frank Tyson and Brian Statham, who were the earth-shattering fast bowlers in the MCC team captained by the late Sir Leonard Hutton.

In the Caribbean, led by Ian Johnson, Australia won the First Test by nine wickets, drew the Second and won the Third in Georgetown by eight wickets in only four days.

When we played the Fourth, in Barbados, we made 668 and had West Indies in all kinds of trouble at 147/6 on the third evening. It looked a 'lay down misère'.

Assume nothing in this game.

The next day, the overnight not-out batsmen, Denis Atkinson (219) and Clairemonte Depeiza (122), batted throughout the five hours' play, Atkinson with some lovely strokes and Depeiza with his nose and his bat touching the pitch. Nothing got past, not even the ones which kept low. Clairemonte and the horizontal defensive stroke were inseparable that day.

The next morning I bowled to Depeiza, he lifted his head, balanced on one leg, essayed a flamboyant back-foot drive and the ball ran straight along the ground and bowled him.

In 1991, when I was working on television for Channel Nine in the Caribbean, I was in Barbados and just about to host the 'intro' to the one-day game eventually won by the Australians to give them that Limited-Overs series. No one knew at that time Australia were about to win. The crowd was in high good humour. They knew they were in for an exciting game, and some were even celebrating and toasting their heroes pre-match. Loudly!

At least one of them also had his cricket history in good shape.

In my earpiece the Director's voice said, 'Fifteen seconds to on-air' and there was, for some reason, a momentary hush around the ground, with drums and cymbals silenced. As if on cue, came a very loud, and very Bajan voice.

'Hey, Sir Richard Benaud,' it echoed around the small ground.

Now he had everyone's attention.

'You de son of dat guy who couldn't get out Atkinson and Depeiza all de fourth day in 1955?' I managed a quick and slightly tight smile to acknowledge the minor connection, even if he did have the family line slightly astray.

'If you couldn't bowl dem out, you do right to take up television, man,' he continued, just as I was saying, 'Good morning and welcome to the paradise island of the Caribbean.'

But I was saying it through my own laughter and that of a thousand spectators in the Kensington Stand right behind me.

The man's timing was perfect, and so was his memory.

BOB BEVAN

—◄◦►—

What can one say about Bob The Cat that he has not said already? He is not only the old Wilsonians greatest ever 6th-XI goalkeeper, but also one of Britain's greatest after-dinner speakers. He was for many years a Trustee of the Lord's Taverners.

Last October, I sat in the dressing room before our first round AFA 6th-XI cup-tie. I was resting in between tying up my left boot and my right boot – the doctor has told me not to lace up one immediately after the other – when a young player in the corner piped up,

'Pardon me, Cat, but is this the first round?'

I bit my lip. A tear rolled down my cheek. I tried to catch it, but missed.

'Yes son,' I said sadly. 'We only play in first rounds.'

* * *

In my first game of the 2003 season for Bells Yew Green away to Outwood, it might be fair to say that my fielding was not yet into its usual mid-season sharpness. Our captain,

Mark Beard, who as club treasurer is not generally noted for his humour, said to me, 'I've found out how to hide you in the field.'

'How?' I enquired.

'I'm bringing you on to bowl.'

HAROLD BIRD

—◄○►—

Dickie Bird MBE played county cricket for Yorkshire and Leicestershire and then went on to become our best known and best loved umpire. At the start of his 66th and final Test, at Lord's in 1996, the Indian players stood as a guard of honour as he came out to umpire. He still gave Michael Atherton out lbw in the first over.

I remember umpiring at Old Trafford (everything seemed to happen to me at Old Trafford) in an England v Australia

Test. Bob Holland, the Australian leg-spinner, was bowling from my end to Graham Gooch. Holland bowled a full toss, which Graham hit straight back at me like a bullet. It hit me on the ankle and down I went. The Australian physio came out onto the field to give me treatment, to a huge cheer from the full house at Old Trafford.

After I received my treatment and stood up rather shakily to restart play, Bob Holland thanked me for saving four runs. Graham Gooch, on the other hand, was not happy at having lost four runs. It's amazing what can happen in the middle of a Test match.

NAAS BOTHA

◄○►

South African rugby international, a
former Springbok fly-half and captain during
the 1980s, who scored 312 points
in international rugby.

We were watching an international soccer match at Loftus Versfeld stadium in Pretoria, when after the game I went off and got a bunch of my friends a round of drinks.

As I returned with a tray full of beers, my mobile phone rang, It was my wife, Karen. She wanted to know when I was coming home, so I naturally replied that I was already on my way and wouldn't be long.

I then sat down with my mates and carried on chatting about the football.

My mate Dave looked rather surprised, and he asked, 'Didn't I just hear you tell Karen you are on your way?'

'Yah,' I said, 'but I'm the type of bloke who, if he is going to get into trouble, likes to do it in instalments.'

IAN BOTHAM

◄○►

Perhaps England's greatest all-round cricketer
of all time, Ian Botham is best remembered for his
amazing displays in 1981, when his batting and
bowling transformed lost causes and brought
the Ashes back home. Since his retirement,
Botham has raised millions for charity
by his marathon walks.

I have many great memories of touring with the England team during my cricket career, and numerous stories to tell about my room-mates! However, one man stands out in particular – Derek Randall, or Arkle as he is known to his fellow players and friends.

On returning to his hotel room in Adelaide, following a day in the field, he decided to run a bath. Having turned the water on, he remembered that he needed to pass on a message to Messrs. I.T. Botham and A.J. Lamb. He quickly wrapped a towel around his body and slipped across the corridor to their room. We opened the door to Arkle, invited him in for a drink (a cup of Earl Grey, of course) and spent a while chatting. On leaving the room, he realised that he had left his key inside his room. Unlike most people, instead of asking either Lamby or myself to ring down to reception, he decided to go down himself.

At the Adelaide Hilton that night, there was a rather special function, with people from all over Australia arriving dressed in DJs – the works. As the towel-clad Arkle arrived at the reception desk, there was utter chaos, with people running hell for leather out of the dining room, some soaking wet.

While asking the very flustered receptionist if he could have another key for his room, he also enquired what the problem was.

'Some stupid **** has left their bath water running and flooded the dining area!'

No need to ask who, as she handed over the replacement key to a slightly under-dressed Mr. Randall!

MAX BOYCE

Welsh comedian, raconteur and musician – and rugby
fan. His album We All Had Doctors' Papers *was the*
first comedy album to top the charts.

When I visited Madame Tussaud's in London a few years
ago, I was amazed to see some large life-size wax models of
the Welsh rugby team being loaded into a forty-foot con-
tainer marked 'URGENT – for the attention of the England
selectors, Twickenham'.

I enquired what they intended doing with them and was
told that the English selectors had ordered them and were
going to install them at Twickenham. The England team
were then going to practise tackling and sidestepping them.
Intrigued, I rang the Chairman of England selectors and
asked him how the new training method was going.

'Not very well,' he replied. 'Wales won, 14–6.'

C

GEOFFREY CHATER

*Prolific British character actor who has appeared in
countless films and television dramas, from* If *and*
Gandhi *to* Harry Enfield's Television Programme.
Keen cricketer for the Lord's Taverners.

I was invited, as a young actor and Taverner who played cricket
a bit, to play at Bishops Stortford in August 1953. Godfrey
Evans – Taverners' captain that day – asked if anyone else would
put on the gloves as he had hurt a finger. No hand was raised
except mine, and armed with Godfrey's gloves (I had none with
me) I had to face Denis Compton's chinamen and seamers.

'Not to worry,' said Denis. 'I'll give you a signal when it's
going straight through.'

Needless to say, the signal reception failed quite seriously,
and bye after bye disappeared with me jumping in the
wrong direction. The crowd got the message and started to
laugh: I too was corpsing and the game nearly came to a
complete halt. The situation was saved, I seem to remember,
by Denis taking himself off.

RAY CONNOLLY

*Writer, journalist and novelist, who wrote
the screenplay for two of the biggest British film
successes of the 1970s,* That'll Be The Day
and Stardust. *Also a great authority
on The Beatles.*

There's no pleasing some people. Or, to put it another way, for sports masters, the looniest of all sports fanatics, sport really isn't about winning. At least, it *wasn't*.

As a boy in the Fifties I went to a rugby-mad Catholic grammar school known as West Park in St Helens, Lancashire, where every team in the school was much feared for many miles around.

Naturally a weed like me never got near to being selected for a West Park team. Thank God! But a class-mate and friend of mine, Peter Harvey, who would captain England Schoolboys during his time there, learned very early that it wasn't enough simply to be good to satisfy the rugby master. You had to play with an etiquette which, if not of another planet, was definitely from another age.

He discovered this one Saturday morning when playing for the Under-14s team, the Bantams, against another school. For some reason he was chosen to play at full back and encouraged to practise his kicking by taking the conversions. Uncertain of his kicking ability, however, Harvey asked his team-mates to make sure that if they scored they touched down behind the posts to make the conversions easier for him.

This they duly obliged, often crossing the line at the corner flag and then beating a couple of extra players before touching down between the posts. Every try was converted.

By half-time, when there were something like fifty points to nil on the scoreboard, the senior rugby master, a mad martinet called Dicko, who taught us Latin and who was watching from the touchline, decided that it was becoming embarrassing for the opposition.

As oranges were passed around he went across to the referee, a much junior teacher, and suggested that when the score reached seventy points, the game should be stopped to avoid further embarrassment to the other school. So, into the second half they went. With twenty minutes still to go, and the score reaching seventy–nil, the game ended.

Of the seventy points, Peter Harvey, the boy who was uncertain about his kicking, had been responsible for forty-three of them, scoring five tries himself and kicking fourteen conversions. Naturally he was delighted all weekend, so when on the Monday morning he received a message that he had to report to the rugby master in the gym his expectations were high.

What could it be? Was he to be made the Bantams captain? Or perhaps he was being promoted and would be playing in the Under-16s the following week? Or maybe house colours were to be awarded; at the very least a quarter star.

It was none of these. As he entered the gym Dicko reached for his cane, and very swiftly set about giving Harvey a very hard four strokes on the hands.

With his fingers swelling Harvey gasped: 'But why, sir? What have I done?'

'What have you done, boy?' bellowed Dicko. 'What have you done!! I don't mind you beating inferior opposition. But to ask your team-mates only to touch down between the posts, thus colluding with them to beat two or three players after having crossed the line and so humiliate the opposition is ungentlemanly conduct, and quite unacceptable in the game of rugby...'

Footnote: Of that team of fifteen Bantams, four players, including Harvey, went on to play representational senior rugby for either England or Lancashire, while a further three turned professional on leaving school and played Rugby League for St Helens, Widnes and other Lancashire clubs. Some team!

HENRY COOPER

<o>

Sir Henry Cooper OBE KSG held the British and Commonwealth heavyweight titles from 1959 to 1970, and was also three times European heavyweight champion. His left hook, known as 'Enery's 'Ammer', was a feared weapon, which put Muhammad Ali on the canvas for the first time ever, in 1963.

I was driving my car accompanied by my former manager, Jim Wicks (who was at that time about 17 stone) and my twin brother George, when a gentleman on a bicycle suddenly pulled out in front of me. As he did so, I quickly braked, but unfortunately he fell off his bike.

I pulled over to see that he was not hurt, and wound my window down to ask if he was OK. He came over to me and gave me a right back-hander. With that, Jim Wicks, my brother George and I all got out of the car and looked at the gentleman, who must have weighed about

8 stone. He looked at me and said, 'You think you're brave, just because there are three of you!'

BOB COTTAM

Hampshire, Northamptonshire and
England fast bowler, who took 9 for 25
against Lancashire at Old Trafford in 1965,
then the best bowling figures by any
Hampshire player.

Imagine the scene – a beach bar in Barbados. The England Under-19s are touring and the sun is setting. It is a most beautiful evening.

The barman had only one arm, having lost the other in a motorcycle accident, but he mixed wonderful cocktails, and was extremely efficient and quick. Just as we began our meeting, one of the lads sank back in his chair, stretched out and said, 'This must be paradise. Most people would give their right arm to be here.'

Eventually the barman saw the funny side too.

* * *

During my first year at Hampshire, I was batting in the nets and an old guy in a flasher's raincoat and trilby hat kept commenting on my technique, or lack of it. As I replaced the off-stump for the umpteenth time, I was awaiting his comment. Sure enough, he didn't let me down.

My response was to tell him to eff off, at which point he informed me he was Harry Altham, President of MCC and

43

Hampshire. I spent the next week picking up paper under the seats.

How times have changed.

YOUR LEFT ARM'S BENT... YOUR RIGHT LEG'S TOO FAR FORWARD...

STEPHEN COVERDALE

◀─◦─▶

*Chief Executive of Northamptonshire
CCC from 1986 to 2004*

I was playing golf with a friend who has a reputation as a man with an eye for the ladies, and who really

44

fancies himself as a golfer. He was playing badly. The more he tried, the worse he got, and the more his temper increased. Off the 17th tee, he pulled his shot far left, fully 50 yards out of bounds. Furious, he put a second ball down, and gave it an almighty whack. That ball he sliced horribly; it hit a tree and rebounded way, way out of bounds to the right.

Immediately he pulled out another ball, but before he took his next attempt, I thought I would calm him down with some advice.

'Slow down. Take it gently. Imagine you're making love to your secretary.'

Back came the immediate response, 'How the hell do you think I can hit a golf ball with a paper bag over my face!'

CHRIS COWDREY

<>─

Son of Colin, Chris Cowdrey captained both Kent and England at cricket. In a first-class career stretching from 1977 to 1992, he scored over 12,000 runs and took 200 wickets. He is now a cricket journalist and broadcaster.

You will probably be aware that between my father Colin and me, we captained England on 31 occasions. I can't remember the exact split, but I seem to recall that he was around the 30 mark.

JOHN CRAWLEY

*Cambridge University, Lancashire, Hampshire
and England batsman, who made his Test debut
for England in 1994.*

The setting is a post-season tour to Jersey with Lancashire. It was a very friendly game, during which Andy Flintoff got hit in the private parts, obviously without a box on. He was carried off, and in the privacy of the dressing room used a pint glass to soothe the affected area.

It was a very hot day, and Gary Yates had been batting a long time. He was finally out, and on his return to the pavilion, immediately looked for refreshment. Dressing rooms being what they are, everybody pointed him in the direction of the offending pint glass. He supped the whole lot down. The dressing room erupted with laughter and sniggering. Gary's reaction is, unfortunately, unprintable.

ROBERT CROFT

—◄○►—

*Glamorgan and England cricketer, off-spinner and useful
lower order batsman, who has played more Tests for
England than any other Glamorgan player.*

Hugh Morris (while captain of Glamorgan CCC) and Graham Gooch were interviewed about their hopes for the 1993 season.

Hugh's hopes were to score 1,000 runs, for Glamorgan to finish tenth in the County Championship, tenth in the Sunday League, and to reach the first round of the Nat West and Benson and Hedges Cups.

Graham's hopes were for 1,500 first-class runs, 1,000 Test runs in the calendar year, 35 first-class wickets, not to mention Essex winning the County Championship and the Nat West Cup, finishing in the top three in the Sunday League, and reaching the final of the Benson and Hedges Cup.

He added, 'I'm also feeling very fit and hope to do the London Marathon in under three hours.'

The interviewer then said, 'Isn't that a bit optimistic, Graham?' to which Graham replied, 'Well, Hugh bloody started it!'

BARRY CRYER

—◄○►—

Comedian, star of BBC radio's I'm Sorry
I Haven't A Clue, *comedy script writer and
brilliant after-dinner speaker.*

My membership number of the Lord's Taverners is 1066, so I hope I can be allowed an archery story.

The night before the Battle of Hastings, King Harold was inspecting his archers. He painted a target on a barn door, and told his archers to demonstrate their prowess. The first bowman fired an arrow and pinned a butterfly to the barn door in the middle of the target. The second threw a clod of earth in the air and pierced it with three arrows before it too was pinned to the door. The third fired, missed the barn door, and everybody was forced to duck when his arrow ricocheted off a tree.

'Watch out for this one,' said the King. 'He'll have somebody's bloody eye out in the morning.'

* * *

Willie Rushton, on checking into the Europa Hotel, Belfast, read on the registration form the question, 'How did you hear about this hotel?' As it had been blown up three times, he wrote, 'News At Ten'.

D

DICKIE DAVIES

--◆◇◆--

The one-time face of ITV Sport, and long-serving presenter of World Of Sport, *Dickie Davies is a legend in sporting journalism.*

Some years ago, Welsh rugby was going through some very bad times, and the team was beaten by the likes of Romania and Canada. The result was that the Welsh RFU just couldn't sell any tickets for the games. So they tried new outlets, like a chemist's shop in Llanelli. Gwyn and Gareth passed by and saw the ad in the window for tickets for the next Wales game. Because of their desire to support their country, Gwyn went into the chemist's to buy two tickets, while Gareth waited outside on the pavement to check that nobody they recognised came by.

Eventually, Gwyn came out again, carrying two packets of condoms.

'What do you want those for, Gwyn?' asked Gareth. 'You don't know any women.'

'No, but I was too embarrassed to ask for the tickets.'

GARETH Y DAVIES

Head of Sport at S4C.

Clive Rowlands captained Wales in all of his 14 appearances. He then became national coach, President of WRU, and was manager of the successful British Lions tour to Australia in 1989.

He is often remembered as the scrum-half who 'kicked the leather off the ball', and was largely responsible for 111, yes 111 line-outs in the Scotland v Wales match at Murrayfield in 1963 which Wales won 6–3. As a result of this, the laws were changed within a short time, to prevent a player kicking the ball directly into touch outside the respective 22-metre areas.

Six years or so ago, whilst Clive and I were on broadcasting duties in Edinburgh, *The Scotsman* newspaper carried a full page on famous Scotland v Wales matches, with photographs of Gerald Davies, Andy Irvine and John Taylor, who had all played key roles in some of the memorable clashes between both nations.

At the foot of the page there was also a photo of Clive, and he was quite pleased despite the heading being 'the man who nearly killed the game'!

As we later entered Murrayfield a very enthusiastic steward – we've all met them – approached Clive in a very officious manner and said, 'Pass please', to which Clive instantly responded, 'Don't you read the papers? I never give a pass at Murrayfield!'

KEVIN DEVINE

*Scots broadcaster and former member of
the BBC TV* That's Life *team.*

Celtic supporters are known throughout the world for their friendliness and enthusiasm for the game of football, whenever and wherever they follow their team.

Witness – Seville 2003, UEFA Cup final, Celtic 2–3 Porto.

UEFA decided to give the 'fair play' award for that year to the supporters of Glasgow Celtic Football Club, for their impeccable behaviour and attitude, after 80,000 of them descended on Seville for the final. This is the first time the award has ever been presented to a set of fans rather than a team!

Right from their first forays into Europe and beyond, the supporters have been there in their thousands, to witness the ups and downs of their team, being magnanimous in victory and retaining a sense of humour in defeat.

During the 1990s Rangers were dominant in Scotland, and Celtic were not the force they had been during the Jock Stein era. In the 1996/97 season they faced another early exit from Europe, this time at the hands of Hamburg. After a first-leg defeat at Parkhead, 0–2, Celtic were trailing 2–0 in Hamburg and there was no way back.

The 4,000 supporters who had travelled with them were hopelessly outnumbered and trying to make as much noise as possible in support of their team, but it was the masses of jubilant Hamburg supporters who were raising the roof with the chants of their team's victory.

Then from the middle of the Celtic support came a call asking for the crowd to hush.

'Sssshhhh! Sssshhhhh! Ssssshhhhhh!'

The cry spread throughout the Celtic support and soon they were all putting their fingers to their lips and urgently 'shushing' those around them. Before you knew it the whole of the Celtic support were silent. This was noticed by the surrounding Hamburg fans, who, wondering what the urgency was for the call for hush, very quickly shushed themselves and the whole ground into silence. What had been a raging torrent of triumphalism just moments before, was suddenly as quiet as the grave and you could clearly hear the calls from the players on the park, shouting to each other, as the game went on. Silently everyone waited.

After about twenty seconds of this unnatural, eerie silence the original group of Celtic supporters who had started the call for hush, jumped to their feet and started singing at the top of their voices –

'Can you hear the Hamburg sing, No-o, No-o!

Can you hear the Hamburg sing, No-o, No-o.'

Who ever said that we never had a sense of humour, even in defeat!

PAT DEWES

◄◉►

*Successful South African businessman
and sports entrepreneur, whose first-class
cricket career went by in a flash
in the 1970s.*

This was told by D.H. Robins in an after-dinner speech at the Wanderers, Johannesburg during his team's tour of South Africa in 1974/75.

The Duke of Norfolk was invited to be a guest steward during Royal Week at Ascot. In the parade ring he spied a trainer slip something from his pocket and feed it to a horse.

The Duke strode importantly across the ring and confronted the trainer. 'I say my good man, what was that you fed to the horse just now?'

'Nuffink but sugar Guv'nor,' replied the trainer.

'Let me see,' demanded the Duke, and the trainer produced two more lumps of sugar from the pocket of his coat. He popped one into his own mouth and offered the other to the Duke. Now feeling a little foolish, the Duke swallowed the sugar, turned and left.

The trainer then turned to his jockey to give him his riding instructions.

I HAVEN'T SEEN THE DUKE SO FAST ON SUGAR FOR AGES!

'From the off, I want you to settle her down against the rail and five or six off the pace. When you get into the straight, move her to the outside and give her a couple of reminders with the whip. If anyone passes you after that it will either be me or the Duke of Norfolk.'

* * *

It was a typical stifling February day in Durban. I was in the slips for my club, Zingari, during a club game against Durban High School Old Boys. Despite the fact that we had pretty much an all-Provincial attack, including the world-class Vince van der Bijl, we were being put to the sword by the DHSOB opening bat, one Barry Anderson Richards.

As yet another awesomely elegant Richards cover drive clattered into the pickets to bring up his 150, Bruce Groves, Barry's former opening partner for Natal, left his position next to me, walked up to Richards and said, 'Give us a kiss Barry.'

'What?' responded Richards. 'Whatever for?'

'Because,' said Bruce, 'I like a bit of intimacy when I'm getting a good f***!'

JASON DODD

━━━━━◄○►━━━━━

Long-serving captain of Southampton FC,
who played over fifteen seasons with Southampton,
having been signed from Bath in 1989.

The Art of Football Management
Coming into the dressing room after a defeat is not a nice feeling. After one game, Chris Nicholl the

manager was going mental at us when somebody outside leant on the light switch, plunging us into darkness. Seconds later, the light came back on, to reveal the Boss in boxing pose, hands up and ready to jab. His words were, 'Well, you had your chance and I was ready.' He thought the boys had planned to turn off the light and were going to jump him! Being a big chap, he wouldn't have had any problems with that, especially from me!

NEIL DURDEN SMITH

◄○►

'Durders Of Course' (so named as the
answer to the question 'Who was at the
party/reception/dinner/premiere last night?')
was a member of the Test March Special team
in the 1960s and 1970s, and was involved
in the conception and establishment of
the Rugby World Cup. He is a former
chairman of the Lord's Taverners.

I have to admit to feeling partly responsible for the West Indies being bowled out for by far the lowest score in their history, at least until England got hold of them in Jamaica in early 2004. Let me explain.

In my days as a broadcaster I was quite often invited to go to Ireland to be the commentator for BBC's outside broadcasts, on both television and radio. In the summer of 1969 I was asked to cover the historic televised inaugural one-day cricket match between Ireland and the West Indies at Sion Mills, a tiny Ulster town in Co. Derry. How historic it turned out to be!

Tuesday 1st July was the last day of the Lord's Test and England batted all day, Boycott scoring 106 and Sharpe 86. I was in the *Test Match Special* team in those days, alongside John Arlott and Brian Johnston, and that evening I went to Heathrow with the West Indies party from St John's Wood to catch the flight to Belfast. We were met at Aldergrove by a fleet of cars and driven to a hotel in Londonderry where we were to spend the night. After dropping off our bags, we all went out to dinner at a Chinese restaurant. I remember thinking then that it was slightly incongruous being with a collection of cricketers from the Caribbean tucking into sweet and sour pork and fried rice in a Chinese restaurant in the Emerald Isle, having completed a Test Match at Lord's that very afternoon!

The following morning, Wednesday 2nd July, dawned cloudless and sunny. Gary Sobers, captain of the touring side, had decided in his wisdom to take a few days off to go racing and Lance Gibbs, the vice-captain, had bowled 41 overs in England's second innings at Lord's, so his spinning finger resembled a piece of raw steak and there was no way he could play. Basil Butcher, the next senior player, was appointed captain for the match and Clyde Walcott, the manager, was pressed into service (not a bad former player to have in your side!). I travelled to the ground in the same car as Butcher, Gibbs and Walcott. Basil asked me en route what he should do if he won the toss. 'You must bat,' said I, 'because if you field first and bowl Ireland out before lunch there won't be a match worth watching.' I was not to know my pearls of wisdom were to lead to utter disaster for the West Indies!

The beautiful Sion Mills ground, with a river running down one side of it, was absolutely packed. The outfield looked immaculate and, due to some overnight rain, the wicket was fittingly emerald green and slightly damp to boot. That didn't stop Butcher electing to bat after he had won the toss, and at 11.30 Steve Camacho and Joey Carew walked out to open the innings. In Dougie Goodwin, the captain, and Alex O'Riordan, Ireland had a pair of opening bowlers good enough to have played first-class cricket, had they been interested. They bowled brilliantly, so brilliantly that after 40 minutes the West Indies – Butcher, Lloyd, Foster, Walcott, Shepherd et al. – were 12 for 9. At that point a little-known fast bowler (then as now) called Blair came in at number 11 to join Shillingford. Together they scythed at every ball and somehow they managed to score another 13 between them, Shillingford finishing with 9 not out, by far the highest score of the innings. So the mighty West Indies had been humbled for 25, Goodwin taking 5 for 6 and O'Riordan 4 for 18, with one bye and one run out. It could so easily have been 12 all out. Ireland duly won by nine wickets and the West Indies sportingly agreed to carry on and play a beer match for the benefit of the huge crowd crammed into the idyllic little ground. They made many friends by doing so and they took their defeat with great charm and good humour. How it must have hurt, though!

On a personal note I will never forget my day at Sion Mills. The commentary box was just that: a box perched dangerously high up on top of a Heath Robinson contraption, laughingly described as scaffolding. The only way up was via a flimsy ladder – rather like going up the north face of the Eiger, I imagine. There was just room in the box for one other person, the producer. The scorer was a lady sitting in a deck-chair at ground level and the bowling figures (thereweren't many runs) had to be hauled up to me at the end of each over in a bucket on the end of a rope. I thanked my lucky stars for a strong bladder, because I was stuck in that box for hours doing pieces into seemingly endless radio and television programmes. It was even the lead story on the one o'clock news bulletins!

My days of proffering advice to touring teams on how to proceed when winning the toss are definitely over!

E

JANE EAGLEN

<o>

Dramatic soprano famed for her portrayals of
Wagner's heroines, and an avid cricket enthusiast.

The Royal Northern College of Music was and is a wonderful place to study music and, in my case, singing. It had some great teachers and facilities, and it had the great advantage of being in Manchester, home of Old Trafford Cricket Ground.

In my first year at college, I was so excited to be living in a place where first-class cricket was played that I was determined, no matter what, to see some matches.

The perfect opportunity was a One-Day International game, to see England play the old enemy Australia. I made my excuses to various classes that I was not feeling well, and off I went armed with a few sandwiches and water, and most important of all, some suntan oil, as the forecast was for a hot day.

The day was indeed hot, and the cricket excellent and absorbing, so I simply slathered on the oil and cheered England to a close victory. As I was there alone, I passed a few comments with people sitting close by, discussing the bowling and fielding and the unusually hot Manchester day.

I left Old Trafford happy to have seen a great game, and barely noticed that my arms and face were a little warm, and that children seemed to be pointing and looking scared in my general direction. I took the bus back to my hall of residence, and walked into the reception where a group of people were talking. Silence fell as I passed, so I smiled and carried on. As I walked past people in the corridor the same look of horror was evident, though still it didn't occur to me why.

I reached my room, and happened to glance in the mirror, at which point it all became painfully clear what had happened. I was the colour of an over-boiled lobster, with snow-white rings round my eyes where my sunglasses had been. My nose raised the temperature of the room several degrees and my arms were starting to throb.

The following day, after little sleep, my eyes wouldn't open and my forehead was swollen to something resembling the Elephant Man. I had to visit the doctor, who was not convinced I hadn't burnt myself on a kettle rather than the sun. It took several days before I could go out at all, and for the rest of the summer I remained out of the sun. In fact I have pretty much done so since that day.

I still believe it was worth it to see England triumph!

ROD EDDINGTON

<o>

Not only Chief Executive of British Airways, but also twelfth man for Oxford v Cambridge at Lord's in 1976.

I lived in Japan for four years and played cricket at the Yokohama Country and Athletic Club near Tokyo. I was one of a small band of expatriate cricketers who played in Japan, mainly Brits and Aussies.

One of the sides we played against had a Japanese player who bowled perfectly respectable leg breaks. I quizzed him at tea as to where he had learnt this difficult art.

'I spent some time at school in Britain and became a real fan of the game there,' he said.

I suggested that it was very unusual for a Japanese man to feel so strongly about our great game, particularly as baseball had such a strong following in Japan.

'Not at all,' he replied, with a perfectly straight face. 'We Japanese love the game of cricket so much we even put the ball in the middle of our National Flag!'

Only in the Orient, I thought.

FRANCES EDMONDS

—◄○►—

Writer and broadcaster whose Cricket XXXX Cricket, *describing an England tour which included her husband Philippe, lifted the lid on what goes on when cricketers are on tour – apart from the cricket, of course.*

On the 1987 cricket tour of Australia, there was the usual avalanche of Aussie 'sledging'. One of the most verbal was wicket-keeper Tim Zoehrer, whose keeping was not quite in the same league as his invective. I therefore penned him a limerick. He replied with one directed to my husband, Phil.

FROM FRANCES EDMONDS TO TIM ZOEHRER:
There was a young glove-man called Zoehrer
Whose keeping got poorer and poorer.
Said AB* from first slip

'Please stop giving such lip,
And with extras stop troubling the scorer.'

*Allan Border, the Australian captain

FROM TIM ZOEHRER TO PHIL EDMONDS:
There was a balding old man named Phillippe
Who stands in the gully too deep.
When his turn came to bat
He opened his trap
And his innings just fell in a heap.

BELLA EMBERG

◄○►

*Actress and comedienne, known especially for her part in
Benny Hill's television programmes.*

I bought a card a few years back when the English Test team
were regularly dismissed for very low scores. The message
read:

'What do an average male and an England cricketer have
in common? It's a miracle if any of them stay in longer than
five minutes!'

It made me laugh, and it still does, but the best news is
that England have outlived that gag. And Brian Lara may be
a great cricketer, scoring his wonderful 400 not out, but does
it always have to be against England. Can't he pick Australia
next time?

F

THEO FENNELL

━━━━━━━━━━━━━━◄○►━━━━━━━━━━━━━━

*Distinguished jeweller and schoolboy cricketer who
played twice for Eton against Harrow at Lord's.*

A.A. Milne told the story of a very poor club wicket-keeper
who longed to be known as a fine batsman. When playing
against one particular club, he noticed that any batsman
who had scored a century had a little shield screwed onto
the back of his bat, with the score and the opposition's name
engraved on it. A man with three shields, with legends such
as '127 not out v I. Zingari' and '144 v The Army', would
naturally be noticed, especially by the wicket-keeper and the
slips as a very fine batsman.

The wicket-keeper persuaded his club that they, too,
should institute this particular custom, and soon several of
their players had these tiny shields screwed to the shoulder
of their bats. But the keeper, whose lifetime highest score
was only 12, failed to qualify for one.

Eventually he could stand it no longer. He went through
his drawers at home and discovered a shield of the right size

and shape, which bore the legend 'For rescuing three men from drowning at sea'. It wasn't quite what he needed, but he thought that only sharp-eyed wicket-keepers and slips would read the words – all the rest would just assume he had hit a hundred at some time.

He went out to bat for the first time with his new shield on the back of the bat. As he took guard, he heard the wicket-keeper say to first slip, 'He's not much of a batsman, but he's a very brave English gentleman.'

KEITH FLETCHER

◄○►

Essex and England batsman and captain,
and also a former England coach, Fletcher scored
almost 38,000 runs in his career, and hit 63
hundreds. He played for England 59 times
between 1969 and 1982.

It was in the early days of sponsorship, and Essex were due to play Middlesex the next day. We arrived at Lord's to find a large notice in the dressing room saying 'NO TRACK SUITS ALLOWED ON THE PLAYING AREA'.

Essex, wearing our first sponsored track suits, had wandered down onto the hallowed turf to start fielding practice. Col John Stephenson, then secretary of MCC (a delightful man) saw us from his office window and announced over the tannoy, 'No track suits to be worn on the playing area. Please remove your track suits.'

We all dutifully removed the offending apparel to reveal cricket whites, all, that is, except Ray East, who had nothing on AT ALL under his track suit.

The Colonel, still on the tannoy and in his best Oxford accent, said 'Sensibly!'

Ray departed to the pavilion to don his whites.

We and the Colonel found it very amusing.

DICK FRANCIS

<o>

A great National Hunt jockey who almost won the 1956 Grand National on the Queen Mother's Devon Loch, Dick Francis has gone on to become one of the most successful thriller writers of his time.

After the war, I left the RAF and went into horse-racing, joining the stable of George Owen at Cholmondeley in Cheshire as amateur jockey, assistant trainer and general dog's-body. It was George's practice to feed the horses late at night when it was quiet. When George was away at the horse sales, it was my responsibility to go round with the feed trolley and 'put the horses to bed'. One such night, I found an animal down in his stable sweating profusely, eyes wide in pain. The horse had colic which can often be fatal, especially for a horse lying down. I sent for the vet and between us we managed to get him up on his feet. I spent the whole night walking the horse round and round the yard until the colic eased. His name was Russian Hero.

In March 1949, having moved on to another stable as a professional jockey, I rode a horse called Roimond in the Grand National. Roimond was going really well at the Canal Turn on the second circuit when we were passed by another horse going even better and carrying much less weight. We ran on well but were never able to catch the other horse. We finished second and, yes, we were beaten by Russian Hero who won at 66–1. That night at a celebratory party thrown by Russian Hero's owner, Fernie Williamson, I was invited to say a few words about the winning jockey, Leo McMorrow. I stood on a table and recounted the story of how, only a few months before, I had walked the horse around all night to save its life, and finished with the words 'If I'd known what that horse would do to me today, I'd 'ave let the bugger die!'

WILLIAM FRANKLYN

◄◦►

Actor and cricket fanatic who was not only the suave star of the Schweppes advertisements for many years, but has also appeared in The Avengers, Lovejoy *and the Morecambe and Wise film,* The Intelligence Men.

At a services athletic sports competition in 1944, I was selected for the 440 yards. Among the other runners I noticed an RAF aircraftsman with a flash on his shoulder that said JAMAICA. I ran a pretty good race in my best time, but still came second to JAMAICA by at least ten yards.

I continued running and improving my times, and as a member of 3Para, I had done enough jumps to satisfy my legs. The 1948 Olympics were by now my aim.

At the end of 1945 I was recalled from leave to represent the Army. Driving back from Cornwall on a motorbike, I ran out of road at Fleet, in Hampshire, due to unfriendly gravel on a bend. The result was a broken leg, and a nine-month stay in the military hospital at Aldershot. My Olympic hopes were dashed.

The postscript came when I was watching the 1948 Olympics, especially the 400 metres. As the winner breasted the tape, I leapt about on a by now very useable leg, yelling to a few stunned friends, 'That was the bloke!'

'What bloke?'

'The one I told you about, who beat me in the services.'

It was, in both cases, Arthur Wint, the superb gold medal winner. Motor bike or no motor bike, I would at best have come second.

ANGUS FRASER

<o>

Middlesex and England fast-medium bowler
who took 177 wickets for England in 46 Tests, his
career being frequently interrupted by injury. Now
cricket correspondent of The Independent.

In 1994, after scoring 375 against England in Antigua, Brian Lara was given a plot of land by the Trinidadian government, on the side of a hill overlooking its capital city, Port of Spain. Over the next four years, he had a beautiful mansion built on the site. When England returned to the Caribbean in 1998, the First Test in Jamaica was abandoned and both teams rushed to Trinidad to play back-to-back Tests. While the Queen's Park Oval was being prepared, we had some time to kill and Lara invited the England side to his house for a barbeque. Sensing our awe and disbelief at the splendour of the place, he offered to show us around. While doing so, he said that he wasn't quite sure what to do with all the rooms, but thought of naming them after Angus Fraser, Andrew Caddick, Chris Lewis and Phil Tufnell, the bowlers who enabled him to break the world record, because it was us who had allowed him to earn the money to build such a wonderful place.

After the 2004 tour, the extension has a good chance of being called the Harmison, Hoggard, Flintoff, Jones or Batty Wing.

LIZ FRASER

―◄○►―

Comedy actress who has starred in countless films and television shows, notably Hancock's Half Hour, Dad's Army *and the* Carry On *series.*

St Saviour's and St Olave's School for Girls, near the Old Kent Road, had their playing fields in Dulwich. We had the choice of cricket or tennis, and as we were all in love with Miss Robinson, who had either played or been considered for the England cricket team, we all chose cricket! That was a decision I have regretted ever since, as I have never been able to respond positively to an 'Anyone for tennis?'

I was, however, an outstanding wicket-keeper and we won against all opposition – mainly with 'Run Out' on the score-card. I have never seen Miss Robinson since leaving St Saviour's and St Olave's School for Girls, but cricket gave me one important skill to take through life – I can still catch a falling cup before it hits the floor.

G

PAUL GAMBACCINI

BBC radio disc jockey, journalist and author.
World authority on American popular music,
baseball and the comic books of Carl Barks.

In 1965 I was President of my high school student government and my best friend Dick (no jokes, please) was President of the junior class. We played a lot of golf that summer. I remember being on the seventh fairway at our town course and asking Dick if he had heard 'I Got You Babe' by Sonny and Cher, a new entry at number eighteen in that week's WMCA Good Guy Survey. He said he had, and he loved it. I told him it was great, and would be number one in two weeks. And so it was! I don't remember what happened on the rest of the hole.

One day we went to the Westchester Open, which at the time paid the highest purse in America. Every shot meant hundreds, if not thousands, of dollars. Being a weekday, before a weekend of fans and an era of high security, we could roam the course pretty much as we pleased. On one occasion we positioned ourselves for a drive by Jack Nicklaus, the hottest young golfer on the circuit. We got the distance right but, like everyone else, were shocked that he hooked his shot into a gigantic bush. It was 'our bush', so we climbed into it and found the ball. Dick and I sat inside this huge bush waiting for someone to come for Jack's ball. After about half a minute, a head peaked through the greenery. It was the head of Jack Nicklaus! We told him excitedly that it was his ball.

'Thanks, boys,' he said. He took a penalty – no one could take any kind of stance in that shrubbery – and resumed play.

At the time we thought The Bear had been quite the gentleman. I now realise he was also a model of composure, since dropping a stroke while playing for the biggest stakes in the country could not have been a pleasant experience. A lesser man might have been sent into a spasm of verbal intemperance.

LESLEY GARRETT

Operatic soprano whose career has ranged from some of the great operatic roles to easy listening shows on radio and television. Also a sports fanatic.

I sued to be part of the Queen's Head Racing Syndicate based in Epworth in South Yorkshire, a group of about 15 of us including me and my two sisters Jill and Kay, who owned a racehorse called Diva's Delight. The horse was not the most talented thing on four legs, but we loved him.

His main weakness was that he was not good at corners, which is a pity because most courses have corners. He was running at York early in his career – which I have to confess was never meteoric – and was doing really quite well along the back straight. Unfortunately at York there is a sharp bend into the finishing straight. At this point our horse began to drift wide, and the course commentator's voice, to our eternal shame, boomed out, 'If Diva's Delight doesn't take this bend soon, he'll be running along the A1.'

He did manage the corner – just – but came in last.

MIKE GATTING

<o>

Captain of Middlesex and England, who brought back the Ashes from Australia in 1986/87. He played 79 times for England, and scored over 4,400 runs. He hit 94 first-class centuries and scored 36,549 runs in a career that ran from 1975 to 1998. He became President of the Lord's Taverners in 2004.

Sebastian Coe turned up at the Grace Gates at Lord's, with a ticket for England v Australia. It was 10.50 a.m., and the umpires were about to walk out to get the match under way. Seb had not seen the first day of a Test match before, and was desperate to get in to see the first ball bowled. His ticket, however, was for the North Gate, on the other side of the ground, and the gateman at the Grace Gates would not let him in.

'Please let me in here,' said Seb, 'or else I will miss the first ball.'

'No sir,' said the gateman. 'Your ticket is for the North Gate, around the other side of the ground.'

Seb does not like to throw his weight around but by this time he was desperate to get in. So he said to the gateman, 'Do you know who I am?'

'No,' said the gateman.

'I am Sebastian Coe, the Olympic gold medallist and world record breaker in the 800 metres, 1,500 metres and the mile.'

'Oh,' said the gateman. 'Well in that case it shouldn't take you too long to run round to the North Gate.'

I DON'T MIND THE BIKE SO MUCH AS THE HELLS ANGELS GEAR!

DAVID GEMMELL

◄─◦─►

South African sports marketing agent.

I was talking to John McEnroe one year at Wimbledon in the player's bar about a Rolling Stones concert at Wembley which we had both been to the night before. He had been in the VIP area, while I had been down on the pitch.

I asked him how he had enjoyed it. He said he loved the concert but it was very stuffy in the VIP area. But he said things improved when he got to go backstage to meet the band – and mainly because he got to meet Keith Richards. John and I both play the guitar as a hobby, and had often discussed guitarists, guitars and the playing of them. So I said, 'Keith Richards, that's fantastic! Did you ask him to show you a couple of licks?'

He looked at me for a brief moment, and then said quietly, 'Dave, that would be a bit like you asking me for a tennis lesson.'

CALUM GILES

<o>

Ex-England hockey player, who appeared in
143 internationals and scored over 100 goals.

The Champions Trophy, which in 2000 took place in Amsterdam, is a major hockey tournament consisting of the top six ranked sides in the world. We were due to play Spain in the afternoon, and after a light lunch we set off for the match briefing. All of the team piled into the lift for the meeting except one unlucky player, who we laughed at, as missing the lift meant he would be late for the meeting.

Knowing it would be overloaded, we waited as usual for the doors to re-open, ready to laugh at the unlucky ones who would have to exit. Except this time the doors didn't open: under the strain of our weight, the lift had broken. There were 17 of us packed very tight into a lift built to cater for 12 people. We had to wait 45 minutes for the Dutch fire brigade to turn up, and they did eventually let us out, but only in exchange for a hefty fee. We calculated in that time while packed in like sardines that we were approximately 260 kilos overloaded. We also spent 45 minutes trying to convince the hotel staff that it was not our fault, but as the lift doors were prised open and 17 players walked out, our protestations fell on very deaf Dutch ears. Needless to say we missed the meeting, arrived late, played badly and lost 4–0.

IAN GILLAN

<o>

Former lead singer of Deep Purple, and the
original Jesus in Andrew Lloyd Webber and
Tim Rice's Jesus Christ Superstar.

Golf is just another game, isn't it.

I've always enjoyed games and sport. I'm not very competitive and so I don't have the 'edge' which takes the average performer just that little bit further. I'm a great fan of cricket and football, although I do more watching than playing these days. Every now and then, in my sporting prime, I would splatter the stumps with a wicked yorker, or hit a boundary, or take a spectacular diving catch. Actually it was more 'few and far between' than 'every now and then'.

I played in goal on and off for a village police football team over a period of ten years. We normally lost by many goals to nothing, but I would make the occasional stunning save. That save, along with a rare corner (we weren't a complete pushover) gave us the reason to turn up each week, as, at the 'Sunday pint' after the game, we would turn a humiliating defeat into a thoroughly deserved moral victory.

I used to play table tennis at the youth club and I developed a serve that was so fast that I stood back in awe whenever I got one in. Sadly only one in five connected with the other court and they were returned with a ferocity which I considered quite unbecoming, in a friendly game. Bob Marley was impressed with my serve when we used to play at Island Records in the late seventies.

Being good at snooker is regarded in England as the sign of a misspent youth, so out of respect to my mother I was an average snooker player, although I did put in a lot of practice. Later in life things got rather better on the green baize, although I left the long and complicated game behind, and developed a passion for the cunningly hybrid 'English' pool. I even played in a league team for a couple of years until I discovered the captain was drinking my beer.

I was below average at darts, but very consistent. I could be relied upon to score twenty-six every time I approached the oche. I'm average at chess although I love the game. I win as many as I lose but, with great respect to my friends, I'm not sure they present the stiffest challenge.

So what is it about golf that makes me so sickeningly pathetic compared to the lofty average achieved in all other games or sports? I've been playing at the game for twenty-odd years. I'm a member of my local club. I have on occasions played a few consecutive pars. Just when I'm striking the ball cleanly and true the whole thing falls to pieces and oops, there I am on the next fairway or in the pond. Even more embarrassing is the confident swipe with a three iron that gyros thirty feet forward onto the ladies tee. Then there's the putting. When my driving and pitching is comical I putt like a pro, and when I manage to reach the green in regulation ... I six-putt.

It's the advice I've been given, I'm sure of it. Stance, hands, head down, glove (very important to wear one glove, like Michael Jackson), dress code (grrr!), play off the back foot, sand shots, slow down, half swing, you're standing too close to the ball (after I've hit it), practice swing. There's no shortage of advice, all well meant I know, but it conspires to unhinge me. It's a mind thing. All the other games I have played were started as a kick-about, or fooling around in the street where, as a kid, I thought nothing about technique or style but just threw myself into it as an enthusiastic amateur with no thought of success, just a keen desire to play a part. I've had lessons and the teachers have left scratching their heads. I've been on the practice range for hours until every ball is screaming for mercy. I've been told I have great potential when I get it together once in a blue moon, and then someone gives me advice and it all collapses. What am I to do? No, don't tell me ... please.

EVELYN GLENNIE

—◄◇►—

The great percussionist, who has been probably the most in demand soloist in the world for a decade or more, and who has played with all the world's great orchestras.

I was in my back garden indulging one of my favourite pastimes – archery, while being filmed by a German film crew for the Art House cinematic film, *Touch the Sound*. While demonstrating my highly competent abilities, I surprised myself by striking an existing arrow on the target so cleanly that it split like a peeled banana! Shades of Robin Hood! Unfortunately, since the shot was so deft, the film crew decided not to use it.

Later that week, I experienced the other end of the archery spectrum. After finishing my usual round of arrows, I went to retrieve them and a huge gust of wind grasped my home-made target stand, pushing the target forward. All my arrows were completely bowed – they were all ruined!

I now use them to stake plants.

GRAHAM GOOCH

◀◯▶

*One of the all-time greats of English cricket,
Graham Gooch played 118 times for England, including
34 as captain. His 333 against India at Lord's in 1990
was a record score on that ground, and his 456 runs in
the match the most ever scored in a Test match. He
retired in 1997, having scored almost 45,000 runs,
and 128 centuries, at an average of 49.*

At a press conference when I was captain of England, the
conversation went something like this:

Martin Johnson (*Daily Telegraph*): 'You keep losing the
toss.'

Graham Gooch: 'I'm not a very good tosser.'

Martin Johnson: 'It's not you you've got to worry about.
It's the other ten tossers in the England team!'

CHARMIAN GRADWELL

◀◯▶

*Actress known for many television and film
appearances, perhaps most memorably as Jenny
Richards in* Howard's Way. *She also represented
Great Britain as a canoeist.*

At the 1952 Olympics in Helsinki, the great Emil Zatopek
was worried before the Marathon was to be run. He
had never run a marathon before, and did not know how
to pace himself for one. So as the race got under way,
he sought out Britain's Jim Peters, the favourite. Peters
began at a blistering pace, but Zatopek stayed with him,

and asked in his broken English, 'The pace? Is good enough?'

Peters, already worried by his inability to throw off the challenge of Zatopek, replied, 'No, the pace is rather slow.' He thought that Zatopek would exhaust himself too soon if he thought the pace too slow.

Zatopek asked again, mistrusting his understanding of English, 'You are sure?'

'Yes,' replied Peters. So Zatopek raced past him and maintained his higher pace throughout the race to win comfortably. Peters pulled out at 20 miles, his idea of psychological strategy in tatters.

TANNI GREY THOMPSON
——————◄○►——————

Britain's leading Paralympian, multiple gold medallist and multiple winner of the London Marathon, Tanni Grey Thompson OBE is now the Patron of the Lord's Taverners Sports Wheelchair Sponsorship Scheme.

This relates to my appearance on *This Is Your Life*. At the time of the surprise, I had been recording *A Question Of Sport* at the BBC Television Centre. This is an informal programme and everyone dresses casually, so I was wearing jeans and a very casual top. I was convinced that when Michael Aspel appeared with his famous red book, he had come for John Parrott – I had no idea it was for me.

After I had left the *Question of Sport* studio, I was told not to worry about clothes as the team had contacted my husband Ian, who had brought two outfits for me to choose from. I am afraid that Ian has no idea about fashion or colour combinations, and he brought me a green shirt and skirt, a blue jacket and shoes, and a pair of thick brown winter tights. The other 'choice' was even worse. I was forced to wear the green and blue outfit!

That was one night when I really wished that colour television had not yet been invented.

SHEILA GRIER

————◄○►————

Actress whose credits include a long stint in TV's Brookside *(as Sandra Maghie) and* Invasion: Earth.

On a Boy Scout and Girl Guide ski trip in Scotland at the age of twelve, I managed to break a leg. That in itself was not a particularly embarrassing moment, although it did hurt. However, to this day, I still cringe when I remember the way our captain ordered the boys off the bus during our return to Glasgow. She then grabbed somebody's Tupperware lunch-box (empty by this time, I am pleased to report) and told me that as I could not manage the logistics of getting to the loo and then fitting inside the cubicle, I should pee into the plastic lunchbox!

H

JEREMY HANLEY

*Conservative MP and Party Chairman under
John Major, with a strong show business pedigree.
Sir Jeremy's father was the actor Jimmy Hanley
and his mother the actress Dinah Sheridan.*

From 1990 to 1993, I was honoured to be the Under-Secretary of State for Northern Ireland. We worked all the hours that God sent, but the need to relax, exercise and enjoy oneself was still important, even at a particularly tricky time in the province's history. Happily, a Government Minister could always find a four for golf – his two security guards and his Private Secretary (the 'Bernard' to his 'Hacker').

One sunny evening, we reckoned we could grab a quick nine holes at Clandeboye, near Bangor. I drove off and, as usual, hooked the ball into the deep rough down in a woody hollow, about 150 yards from the tee. To save time, I set off to try to find the ball, with Stevie, my lead escort, executing a perfect drive towards the green. As

I got down towards the trees, I heard what was quite clearly the click of an Armalite cocking, from behind the clump.

Trained in such matters, I immediately threw myself flat on the ground and shouted the code word, 'Stevie!' and he charged towards me, throwing his clubs in the air, grabbing his Heckler from his bag as he ran. A second later, my ball came from behind the nearest tree and made a gentle arc onto the fairway. From behind the thicket, a squaddie in full camouflage appeared, and said, 'We can't have Ministers charging around the undergrowth in Northern Ireland, sir.'

He then blew a whistle and down the length of the fairway five more soldiers emerged from the rough, clearly moving from hole to hole ahead of us.

I seemed to end up on the fairway pretty regularly after that, and suffice it to say, that was the first and only time I broke 50 for the outward nine.

TANYA HARFORD

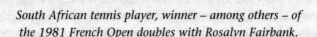

South African tennis player, winner – among others – of the 1981 French Open doubles with Rosalyn Fairbank.

I was playing Martina Navratilova, number 1 seed at Wimbledon in 1979, the opening match on centre court. I had qualified, and so I was really nervous.

At Wimbledon, all players were given new sets of sponsored clothing, and generally never got to wear them before stepping out onto the match court. I was especially proud of my new apparel, some slinky Italian skirt and shirt (all white, of course – Wimbledon didn't allow any colour in

86

those days). I got through the warm-up with no hiccups, even though the Centre Court was by far the largest court I had ever played on. I was so excited as I had aspired to this moment since I was a child.

The first three points were okay – won one point – lost two: thirty–fifteen. Halfway through the fourth point, I had Martina on the run but then, calamity! My skirt's zip came undone, and here I was on Centre Court with the world media and TV focused on me. The question I had to ask myself was should I win the point, but drop my skirt, or grab hold of the skirt but lose the point? Suffice to say there is no photo of me with my skirt around my ankles!!

For the record, I went on to take the first set, but lost the next two, which ended my first Wimbledon experience.

* * *

When I was playing Team Tennis (representing Indianapolis), we were always travelling, and every week it was a new town, city or country, The team used to travel together, three women and three Aussie men, and most of the time we were tired, jet-lagged and generally short on humour.

When, for the twentieth time, the sight of six tennis players each carrying six or eight tennis racquets prompted some obnoxious loud American to storm up to us and enquire if we were indeed tennis players, one of the dry Aussie guys piped up, 'No, actually we are a team of eccentric dildo builders.'

That stopped the conversation there and then.

REVD HOWARD HASLETT

◄○►

Born in Belfast, but from 1973 to 1999 was
Chaplain to Edinburgh Academy, 'exercising there a
pastoral and teaching ministry amongst the cream of
Scotland, all rich and thick'. A rugby enthusiast, in
1986 he was appointed President of Edinburgh
Academicals, Scotland's oldest club.

Several years ago I went with Ian Barnes, the former Hawick and Scotland lock forward, to the town of Elgin in the north of Scotland to speak at the Moray Rugby Football Club's annual dinner.

Just before the formalities were to begin, Barney noticed with consternation that the toast list showed that he was to speak after me, which was not what had been agreed. 'Don't worry,' I said. 'Just tell the President that we've decided to change the order. It won't make any difference.'

So Barney, having been briefly introduced, stood up and delivered his speech, full of hilarious anecdotes, which pulled no punches and left little to the imagination. In due course I followed with my standard offering, and the evening was adjudged a great success.

Next morning, walking down the main street after an excellent breakfast in the town's hotel, Barney was met by a local worthy. 'I thought you were brilliant, last night,' he said. 'But tell me this, your Reverence, do you always swear so f***ing much?'

SCOTT HASTINGS

<><>

Scotland and British Lions rugby player,
with 65 international caps, mainly at centre.

My favourite sporting memory is when Scotland won the Grand Slam in 1990 beating England at Murrayfield on 17th March 1990 by 13 points to 7. Both teams were playing for a 'Winner Takes All' showdown. There was a Calcutta Cup, The Triple Crown, The Five Nations Championship and the Grand Slam to play for. Kenny Milne, Scotland's hooker, advised the BBC in a pre-match interview that he hoped Scotland would win at least one of the titles!

TIM HEALD

<><>

Author of both fiction and non-fiction books, Tim is a
former Chairman of the Crime Writers' Association, as
well as being the author of the official biographies of
Denis Compton and Brian Johnston.

There are endless stories about Denis Compton and I believe most are apocryphal. One of my favourites concerns when, during my 'research' for Denis' biography (which involved a lot of lunch!), Denis turned up at the restaurant looking glum.

'What's the matter?' I asked him.

'Well, old boy,' he said. 'I've just heard they're banning the bands from playing during the cricket at Canterbury Week. The cricketers say it interferes with their concentration.' He then looked thoughtful. 'When I played at Canterbury,' he said, 'I used to try and bat in time to the music.'

If it's not true it should be. And Denis said it.

JIMMY HILL

*Played with distinction alongside Johnny Haynes
for Fulham, led the negotiations with the Football
League that abolished the players' maximum wage,
managed Coventry City with great success and
enjoyed a long and successful career as a TV
pundit. Always controversial, always
informed, often exasperating.*

In the days – or nights – when I fronted *Match Of The Day*, it was customary to remind our audience on the appropriate nights in autumn and spring to adjust their clocks at home, an hour one way or the other depending on the time of year. On one fateful Saturday as winter approached, I dutifully attempted to remind viewers of what they needed to do.

'Don't forget when you go to bed tonight to remember to put your cocks back.'

Alongside me, newsreader Barry Davies snorted loudly with laughter, which collapsed into an off-camera (thank goodness) giggling fit.

RICHARD HILLS

Richard Hills, Director of the Ryder Cup,
has been involved with golf's greatest competition
since the 1980s, and has been instrumental in helping
Great Britain and Europe achieve so much
success during that period.

In 1985 I suddenly realised how popular the Ryder Cup Matches actually were. Within the planning process we had devised a traffic plan, which at the last minute was changed by the police for reasons best known to themselves. It all went horribly wrong and by 9.00 a.m., traffic was queuing from the gates of The Belfry back towards the M6. Drastic measures were called for and we had a tacit agreement with a local farmer that, in an emergency, we could make a hole in his fence and park cars in his field, making use of the green-keeper's JCB.

Our car-parking team was not ready to cope with the extra car park, so another poor mug and I were sent to line up the cars. I was very proud of my car-parking prowess, creating neat lines nose to tail, nose to tail, leaving appropriate gaps to get out. All of a sudden I was confronted by a man in a Hillman Imp, which was old even in 1985, peering at me through a pair of Mr Magoo glasses from his driver's seat. I went into public relations mode.

'Sorry to keep you waiting Sir, hope this will not distract from your day's enjoyment at the Ryder Cup Matches. We are up in two games, level in one, down in one, but you can join them hopefully at the ninth.' To which he replied, in the thickest Brummie accent I have ever heard, 'I did not want to come here. I wanted to do my Mum's shopping in Sutton Coldfield.'

I had no option but to introduce him to my colleague at the other end of the field. 'He is in charge of getting out: I have only been trained to do getting in.'

FRAZER HINES

<o>

Actor, who appeared as Joe Sugden in Emmerdale Farm
*for many years, after having cut his televisual teeth as
one of Dr Who's assistants.*

I was playing a charity cricket match, and had lunch with Michael Holding. I said that I had always hated him when he was bowling against England, and he said, 'Frazer, it's just a game. You bowl the ball as fast as you can to get the batsman out.'

'And then you have a drink with his widow.'

He said, 'Yes, you drink with his ... No! No! You don't want to kill nobody!'

'Aha, Michael,' I said. 'I nearly got you to admit it!'

In reality, Michael is a lovely kind man, and we are firm friends, I'm glad to say.

LIZ HOBBS

<o>

World Water-Ski Racing champion in 1981 and 1983.

At the first World Water-Ski Championships in Italy, having skied my butt off, I was standing to attention on the rostrum, waiting for the National Anthem. But all that came out of the speakers was something that sounded like Pinky and Perky on a bad day.

So I went out to win again in Australia two years later. As I stood on the rostrum waiting, the Anthem started and just as quickly juddered to a halt as the tape broke. Then, from the back of the room, a lone voice began singing, 'God save our gracious Queen ...' The huge crowd joined in, and a lump came to my throat – it was the most moving presentation ceremony of my entire career.

Now, however, whenever I hear the Anthem, I giggle at the memory.

ROY HUDD

━━━━━━━━━━━◄◊►━━━━━━━━━━━

Veteran comic, music hall buff and star of the long-running News Huddlines *on BBC radio.*

On Sundays, my Uncle Bill was a minor league football referee, but on alternate Saturdays he came, with me, to Selhurst Park to see the Glaziers, lately the Eagles, aka Crystal Palace FC.

His missus, my Auntie Ivy, hated football, and try as we might, she wouldn't accompany us. Finally, tired of the Chinese water torture, she succumbed and did come to a match with us.

We stood in the enclosure (a real treat), and with almost the first clearance of the match, the ball ballooned into the crowd, seeking out and hitting – guess who? – Ivy!

She was knocked out, but the St John's Ambulancemen brought her round, and we were forced to take her home. Palace were going through a purple patch at the time and we made it home just in time to hear they'd won, three-nil.

Uncle Bill was not pleased. He commented bitterly, 'What a good job she didn't have her mouth open – they'd never have got the ball back!'

'I 'eard that!' came wafting down from the bedroom. Auntie Ivy never saw another football match.

ANDREW HUDSON

————◄○►————

*South African opening batsman, who was
the first man from his country to score a century on his
Test debut. In all, he played in 35 Tests, scoring over
2,000 runs and hitting four centuries.*

In April 1992, South Africa visited the West Indies for the first time. Having beaten them during the World Cup in New Zealand in February 1992, and having only very recently become international cricketers again, we were not sure what to expect in their backyard.

The tour schedule included three ODI's and a one-off Test match, all jammed into two weeks.

Our first ODI was in Kingston, Jamaica, where Kepler Wessels lost the toss and Richie Richardson asked us to bat. Kepler and I strode to the wicket through a wall of noise, with the local vocal support in full swing. As we walked out, Kepler turned to me and said, 'Why don't you take first strike?' and as the junior partner I had no option but to follow my skipper's suggestion.

I requested guard from the umpire, and then peered down the wicket to the bowler's mark, where Curtly Ambrose was energetically warming up while the crowd began to get behind their man.

First ball, Curtly hurtled towards me, getting taller and taller until he rendered the sight screen useless. He delivered an invisible ball – well that is what I thought – but just to make sure I pulled my head in and closed my eyes. The ball hit the peak of my green helmet and flew high over the head of the leaping wicket-keeper David Williams. After one bounce it crashed into the other sight screen with a thud, much to the delight of the locals.

As all fast bowlers do after bowling a lethal short delivery, Curtly followed through to within centimetres of me and glared down at me from his obvious height advantage.

Then in a deep West Indian voice he said, 'Welcome to the West Indies.'

For the record, the West Indies won all three ODIs and the one-off Test!

SIMON HUGHES

<o>

Middlesex and Durham opening bowler,
who since his retirement has become a respected
journalist and broadcaster. This story was
submitted by his father, Peter.

Middlesex were playing away in a county match. One of the umpires was Dickie Bird, who was staying in the same hotel as the Middlesex team. Dickie had not previously sampled the delights of a Jacuzzi, and Simon showed him how it all worked.

Next morning, Simon was opening the bowling. Running in, he was just approaching his delivery stride when Dickie stuck out his arm and stopped him.

'That were great, that bubble bath last night, Yozzer!' he said.

It took some time for Simon to be in a fit state to carry on bowling.

JENNY HULL

Television newsreader and presenter of
How Do They Do That?

I don't always quite get my facts right.

After dinner one evening with former England footballer Russell Osman and his wife Louise, I decided to mention the fact that Russell had been in a film (the film being *Escape To Victory* starring Sylvester Stallone and Michael Caine, made in 1981).

'Russell, I gather you were in a film – *The Great Escape*. Which one were you up the tunnel? And was Steve McQueen a nice man?'

He said, 'I'm not that old!'

I laughed and I think he thought I was joking! Sadly, I was being serious.

At least I've held on to my dignity.

Has anybody lost an arm?

The wicket is a little damp at the Pavilion End.

The manager said he wants us to give the ball a hoof.

He looks a bit stringy, but what the hell, I'm still hungry.

ABOVE No. The 'C' stands for *Clark Carlisle*.

RIGHT Freddie's nose is picked for England again.

Make up your mind! You can't sit on the fence for ever.

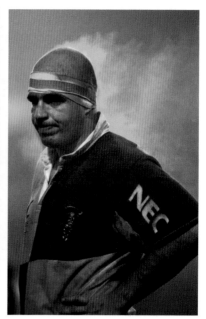

Mary Pierce has always been hungry for success.

The Harlequins forward had a reputation for being a hothead.

I suppose a puck is out of the question.

The England selectors attempt to leave the Oval incognito.

Keep that pose, Lleyton. I'm right behind you.

E.T. Phone home!

Not my face! Not my face!

Ha Ha! That's hilarious! It's the way you tell them!

I feel such a tit. I could have sworn the match was today.

I

COLIN INGLEBY-MACKENZIE

◄◦►

*Captain of Hampshire in 1961, the first
time they won the County Championship, and
president of MCC in the 1990s.*

I had entertained Denis Compton to lunch during a Test
match at Lord's. After lunch we strolled round to the ground
(I live behind the pavilion), and behind the pavilion we
noticed Geoffrey Boycott and David Gower in a keen discussion. They were discussing how many first-class hundreds
each had made. Geoffrey said, 'I told you I've made more
than you!'

Denis Compton quickly retorted, 'And thank God I've
only seen three of them.'

We strolled on.

J

ANTHONY JEFFERSON

————◄○►————

Britannic Assurance chief executive, from 1979 to 1996.

Although we (Britannic Assurance) were the sponsors of the County Championship during the 1980s and 90s, the actual trophy which the winners received had been donated by the Lord's Taverners.

As HRH The Duke of Edinburgh has been the Twelfth Man of the Taverners since the club's formation, it was customary for the trophy to be presented by him to the winners at a ceremony at Buckingham Palace.

When Worcestershire won the Championship in 1988, a date was fixed and on the appointed day we all met up at the Palace. In the party were the winning team and officials from Worcestershire CCC, representatives from the Lord's Taverners, the TCCB and us the sponsors.

Not long before we were due to be received it suddenly dawned on us that no one thought to make sure that the trophy had been brought along. Everyone denied that it was their responsibility and the awful truth emerged that it was still in Nottinghamshire, who had won it the previous year.

It was decided that we had to get a cup from somewhere and as the Taverners office was nearby someone rushed off to see what could be done. In the nick of time they arrived back with a trophy, which was duly presented to Worcestershire CCC by HRH.

And this is how Worcestershire CCC came to be the not-so-proud owners of the 'Billy Cotton Brands Hatch Motor Race Trophy'.

We were led to believe that HRH was not overly amused and it was made sure that the same thing wouldn't happen again.

CHARLES JEFFREY

<o>

Captain of Chelsea Nomads Cricket Club.

On a flaming hot day in the height of an English summer, in front of a large crowd (most of whom preferred to gambol in the stream beside the ground rather than watch the cricket), the Chelsea Nomads were locked in battle against Tilford CC at Tilford.

It was midway through the CNCC's innings when the Tilford paceman sent down a delivery slightly short of a length that bounced about waist-high to the batsman. The batter, who had his eye well in, executed a vicious hook shot, sending the ball at a flat trajectory towards the short leg-side boundary.

The ground at Tilford is on the village green and dips away on that side of the wicket. The whole ground is bounded by small roads which are open to traffic. A car, windows all down in the balmy summer air, was proceeding along that side of the ground where the ball was heading at great velocity. The ball fizzed through the air and entered the car through the open passenger window; it smashed into the driver's nose and exited through the driver's side window, ending up in the stream beyond.

There was a lot of blood and much consternation among the onlookers and, indeed, the fielders. The driver managed to bring the car to a halt, but seemed strangely unwilling to get out of the car, and refused many offers of help.

By this time a sizeable crowd had gathered around the scene of the incident, among which there was a doctor, who quickly diagnosed a broken nose and advised that an ambulance should be called. Emergency services soon appeared, including the police who, as is their wont, started to take down particulars of the driver and the vehicle. It quickly became apparent that the driver was not the owner of the car and was unable to give a satisfactory account of how he came to be in possession of it. The car was indeed stolen, and the police arrested the hapless nasal shatteree in the ambulance en route to the hospital.

Normally when you get a nick in cricket, you are out, but on this occasion he was in – the nick!

JOHN JEFFREY

—◇—

*Scotland back row forward, who won
40 caps for his country and was a member of
the Grand Slam team of 1990.*

I was a guest at the Ladbrokes Gold Cup in Ayr a couple of years ago and while moving between the champagne in the Hospitality Suite and the bookies to place a bet, I was continually getting chatted up by an extremely pretty girl in the public bar.

She knew that I had played for Scotland and she kept making a beeline for me between every race to speak to me and tell me how great I was. Not being one to look a gift horse in the mouth, I accepted her offer of a drink after the last race. Adulation like this does not come very often to me and I was just starting to enjoy it. Then reality dawned as she shouted to her friend, 'Margaret, come and get Colin Hendry's autograph!'

DAVID JENSEN

—◇—

*David 'Kid' Jensen is a veteran radio and
television disc jockey, motor-racing enthusiast
and Crystal Palace fan.*

In 1987, just a few minutes before kick-off, my seven-year-old son Alexander and I were sitting next to each other in our usual seats at Selhurst Park to watch our beloved Crystal Palace.

In front of us was an advertising hoarding for *The Croydon Guardian* with a local headline to illustrate that week's edition of the paper. The banner read 'Brothel Keeper Jailed'. Imagine the hilarity which ensued all around us when Alexander turned to me after several seconds of muttering the word 'brothel' to himself and asked in a loud voice, 'Dad, which division are Brothel in?'

GRAHAM JOHNSON

——◄○►——

*All-round cricketer who played for Kent
between 1965 and 1985, scoring almost 13,000
runs and taking over 550 wickets.*

I am often asked how I set targets as a young cricketer. Well, as I often saw the world from an oblique perspective, I used to set mine from a number of observations. One was set at the Dinner held to celebrate Kent having won the County Championship in 1970. I had played a full season in my first year out of university as Kent rose from bottom in July to the top when it mattered. Among the great and good who attended the euphoric occasion was an icon of Kent cricket – Frank Woolley.

After the dinner, speeches and presentations, Frank rose to leave the room and the entire assembled crowd rose as one to applaud the great man as he walked out. 'That's some target to set myself,' I thought. 'You know you have made it when 600 people applaud your every step as you make your way to take a leak.'

The audience didn't know what to do when Frank walked back into the room!

PS – Still haven't achieved that one – yet.

SALLY JONES

BBC sports journalist, the first woman sports presenter on television, and former world and British real tennis champion.

The well-upholstered Zimbabwe all-rounder and chicken farmer Eddo Brandes was facing Glenn McGrath of Australia in a Test match. He was totally beaten by almost every ball that McGrath bowled at him, but kept getting edges that didn't quite carry to the slips, or making cross-batted swipes that roared through mid-wicket for four. Finally McGrath could take it no longer.

'You ******* fat bloater. You're so **** fat, I don't know how the **** you ever manage to stagger between the wickets. How did you ever get that fat?'

Quick as a flash, Brandes replied, 'Well, every time I sleep with your wife, she gives me a biscuit!'

Play had to be suspended for several minutes to enable the Australian close fielders to stop laughing.

STEVE JONES

——◄◇►——

LBC broadcaster.

In February 1988 I was playing in a charity cricket match at Hampstead. It was LBC v Bertie Joel's XI and we'd got a certain D.I. Gower in as guest ringer. He kept wicket for us!

I'm a left-hander and couldn't find any suitable gear in the bag when it came my turn to bat, so Mr Gower lent me his gloves and his very own bat. You will recall that he had

105

been relieved of the England captaincy in 1986, but I said to him how grateful I was to the *next* England captain for the loan of his stuff. David dismissed the idea.

On the day in question I got into double figures ... not bad with the temperature just above freezing. Almost before you could say 'caught at slip', the selectors had asked David to lead the national side again.

Just call me Mystic Meg.

K

RICHARD KERR

<o>

*Composer of many hit songs, including
'Mandy', a hit for Barry Manilow, Westlife
and many others.*

As a boy, my great hero was Stanley Matthews. When I was about ten years old, I was given a pair of Stanley Matthews football boots, which were for a few days the pride of my life. However, the first time I wore them in a proper game, they split, and could not be used again.

I was so disappointed that I wrote to Stanley Matthews himself, care of Blackpool FC, explaining how his boots had split the first time I used them. Within a few days I got a postcard back from the great man himself, telling me that if I took this postcard and the boots down to the Co-op, he was sure they would replace them free of charge.

I followed his advice, went to the Co-op, and the boots were replaced immediately. I still have the postcard from the great Sir Stanley Matthews, although sadly the boots no longer fit.

RICHARD KERSHAW

◄○►

*BBC television and radio news journalist, a veteran
of programmes such as* Nationwide *and* The World At
One. *Also a keen wicket-keeper batsman for the Lord's
Taverners and many other cricket clubs.*

Ricky Ponting and Shaun Pollock engaged in one of the great sledging matches of recent years. Playing for South Africa against Australia, Pollock had the ball repeatedly going past the outside edge of Ponting's bat.

Pollock told Ponting, 'It's red, it's round and it weighs about 5 ounces.'

Unfortunately for Pollock, the very next ball was hammered out of the ground.

Ponting told Pollock, 'You know what it looks like. Now go and find it.'

JOHN KETTLEY

◄○►

*BBC television and radio weather forecaster and
presenter, immortalised in the 1988 hit single recorded
by the Tribe Of Toffs, entitled 'John Kettley
(Is A Weatherman)'.*

It was a balmy spring evening in 1992 when I was first approached about the possibility of playing for Mrs Major's XI in a charity cricket match at Alconbury.

Although I had already been a Lord's Taverner for two years, playing in similar events with stars of stage, screen and sport, it was clear to me that I should make every effort to accept

108

this exciting opportunity. After all, here was a chance to play alongside my boyhood heroes ... and David English.

So on a perfect afternoon on 24th July, I made my debut at Alconbury under the guidance of former England and Middlesex spin bowler Phil Edmonds. Equally famous colleagues for the day included Jimmy Greaves, Steve Smith-Eccles, Rory Bremner and Joel Garner.

The aforementioned David English was in opposition as usual, and I was to be given a fairly ripe 'cherry' to pit my wits against this dashing left-hand batsman. What came next was near fantasy as English lofted my straight but tempting delivery to deep mid-wicket, only for a slightly overweight Gary Newbon to reel back the years and with amazing athleticism launch himself at the projectile before it reached the boundary.

This was surely one of the greatest catches ever taken in these annual cricket matches and people (well, Gary) have talked about it for years. Obviously I, as the wicket taker, was overjoyed and the fact that I was bowling to such a brilliant field encouraged me to take a further two wickets – though by the end of my spell I was reduced to begging Gary Mason not to hit me!

ROGER KNIGHT

————◄○►————

Formerly a cricketer with Cambridge University, Surrey, Sussex and Gloucestershire, winning four blues and three county caps in the process, Roger Knight is now the Secretary and Chief Executive of the Marylebone Cricket Club.

Some people will remember 1983 when Surrey played Essex at Chelmsford. I was captain of Surrey, won the toss and asked Essex to bat. The pitch was flatter than we had envisaged so we were pleased to bowl Essex out by ten past five for 287. We felt it had been a good day's work from the bowlers.

In the dressing room I told our batsmen that I was not too concerned about runs that evening and we all settled back at the end of a long day to watch Alan Butcher and Graham Clinton start the Surrey innings. With just over an hour to go, our bowlers were quick to take the opportunity of a bath or a shower after a day in the field.

At Chelmsford, the pavilion is at cover point in relation to the wickets, so it is impossible to see from there whether the ball is swinging or seaming. For numbers three and four who were padded up, however, it did appear that Clinton and Butcher were leaving quite a lot of deliveries.

In the fourteen overs of the Surrey innings that evening, the Essex supporters certainly had their money's worth. During those fourteen overs, the atmosphere in the dressing room changed considerably. Batsmen five to eight rushed to prepare to bat, and the bowlers, with much grumbling and moaning, changed back into cricket clothing ready to take a further part in the day's play. At one stage, Surrey were 6 for 6 and then, when the score was 8 for 8, Graham Monkhouse was dropped at slip. At 10 for 9, Sylvester Clarke had a wild heave across the line of the ball and although he did not make solid contact, the ball just crossed the boundary at mid-wicket. At this stage, Pat Pocock, the Surrey no. 11, walked down the pitch and had words with Sylvester, obviously telling him that we were in a very difficult situation and that he should play responsibly. Much chastised, he met the next ball with an immaculate forward defensive up the line of middle and leg, only to lose his off-stump.

At the end of it all, at twenty past six, Surrey were bowled out for 14, the county's lowest ever score. With the scheduled close of play at half past six, there was no further cricket and, as a team, we returned to the County Hotel to consider what had happened.

Although it is easy to say that it only takes ten good deliveries to bowl a team out, one normally expects those deliveries to be spread over a longer period of time. However, if the ten wicket-taking deliveries come early in the innings, a low total is always possible. But the atmosphere in the lounge of the County Hotel that evening is very hard to describe. Shellshock, certainly, a feeling of disbelief and good old British humour in the face of adversity probably summarises the situation best.

Undoubtedly the comment of the evening belonged to the vice-captain, Alan Butcher, who advised us that we needed six more runs in our second innings to avoid an innings defeat by the extras.

The beauty of cricket, though, is that in a two-innings match a batting team has an opportunity to redeem itself, and in the second innings Surrey lost only two wickets in batting out for a draw. At the end of the match, Essex had taken seven points to Surrey's four.

It was a salutary moment for the Surrey team in the year after we had won the NatWest Trophy. It was also a match that those who were playing in the Surrey team will never forget. In fact, we decided to design a tie on which seven small ducks formed the figure seven, under which it said, 'Chelmsford 1983'. Seven of the team had failed to score in the first innings and Pat Pocock was nought not out. Indeed, he was unhappy that he did not qualify for one of the seven ties, as he had not been dismissed.

ALAN KNOTT

—◄◇►—

One of Kent and England's greatest wicket-keepers,
he played 95 Tests for England, scoring 4,389 runs at
32.75, including five centuries, with 269 victims
behind the stumps, still by some distance
the English Test record.

During the 1981 fifth Test, England v Australia, at Old
Trafford, Ian Botham conned me. I had just caught Martin
Kent, cutting at John Emburey. As Dennis Lillee came out to
bat, Alan Curtis, who for years has done the public announce-
ments for Tests, made an announcement which I didn't hear.

I asked Ian about it and when he said that it referred to
some sort of record for Dennis Lillee, I started clapping.
Then Ian revealed: 'You've just obtained the record for
wicket-keeping victims against Australia.'

A voice from the crowd shouted, 'Stop showing off,
Knott,' because I was clapping myself. Ian Botham had really
caught me out!

BURT KWOUK

—◄◇►—

Veteran actor, probably best known for his role as
Inspector Clouseau's lethal assistant Cato in the Pink
Panther *series of films. He also featured in two Bond*
movies, Goldfinger *and* Casino Royale.

In 1959, I was a fairly recent arrival to these shores from the
USA, where I had been a total baseball fan and wholly unin-
formed about the way of life that is cricket.

Appearing with me at the Haymarket Theatre in London at this time were two English actors, Robin Hunter and Tony Kenway. They decided to educate me.

They took me regularly to Lord's where, standing in front of the old Tavern, they would loudly explain the game to me and anyone else within earshot.

'No Burt, that is not a foul ball. That is third man.'

'Oh. And where are first and second?'

'Don't be silly, Burt.'

Thus began my great fondness for cricket, which continues to this day.

L

RENTON LAIDLAW

◄○►

*Golf writer, broadcaster and journalist, one of
the great authorities on his sport. For many years, he
has been television's voice of the European Tour, and
he was recipient of the 2003 PGA Lifetime
Achievement Award in Journalism.*

Filing stories to our newspapers in the early days of the
European Tour was a nightmare. To make a reverse charge
call from Madrid to London was very difficult and involved
going through Paris. Often calls were misdirected and once,
in Madrid, the reporter for *The Observer* discovered he was
telephoning his copy to the *Sunday Mirror*. He only found
out when the *Sunday Mirror* copytaker queried the content of
the story, pointing out that the correspondent was
continually using words that would take up three lines in
the tabloid!

TIM LAMB

<o>

Chief Executive of the England and Wales Cricket Board
until 2004, having played first-class cricket for Oxford
University, Middlesex and Northamptonshire.

I am not sure how many times I played against Yorkshire during my first-class career, but I will never forget some of the fun and games that went on in the margin of these encounters. Like the time when John Hampshire and Colin Johnson went on a batting 'go slow' at Northampton in protest at Geoffrey Boycott having, yet again, taken 90 out of the statutory 100 overs to score a century.

Or the time when the start of a game at Scarborough was held up by picketing pensioners and handbag-waving women protesting about Boycs' suspension and banishment from the dressing room for, as I recall, speaking out of turn to the press.

But my favourite recollection of playing against the Yorkies was a game which took place in the Parks in the early 1970s when, with Oxford nine wickets down and with about ten minutes to go to the close, with the extra half-hour having been claimed by Yorkshire in anticipation of an emphatic two-day victory, yours truly (who in those days did not know one end of the bat from the other) walked out to bat with instructions at least to save some university face by making the game go into a third day.

Boycs, the Yorkshire captain, wanted to go home: the entire rest of the Yorkshire team wanted to stay an extra night enjoying the divers distractions of an Oxford summer evening. For ten priceless minutes we had the absurd specta-

116

cle of Geoff Cope trying his absolute hardest not to get me out, and of Bluey Bairstow coaching me – pleading with me – from behind the stumps.

'Stick your front leg down the wicket son!' 'Leave this one.' 'Bat behind pad, lad.' 'Don't for Christ's sake cut against the spin!'

Somehow I survived the next four overs or so. The Yorkshire lads virtually cheered me off the field. Boycott was absolutely furious. At least some dark-blue honour had been saved, and Bluey and Co. had (I assume) a riotous night out on the town.

GEORGE LAYTON

◄○►

Actor and writer, a regular in It Ain't Half Hot Mum *and creator and writer of* Don't Wait Up *and* Executive Stress. *His best-selling book of short stories,* The Fib, *is part of the National Curriculum.*

It's 1975. I'm in Manchester filming a television series written by two brilliant writers, George Layton and Jonathan Lynn and starring two fabulous actors, George Layton and Jonathan Lynn. We are on the seventh and final episode so you will understand why my mind, my energies, my whole being is focused on only one thing: making sure that this baby of ours, lovingly conceived months before, is delivered safe and well. *You* might understand but the radio producer, who for several days has been vainly leaving messages asking me to call her, doesn't.

'George, I've been leaving messages all over the place! Why didn't you call me?'

These are the days before instant contact. No mobiles, no text messages, no email. Answer-machines are a novelty, fax machines a miracle. Scribbled notes telling you to ring your agent, your wife or irate radio producers are handed to you during rehearsals, stuffed into trouser pockets and forgotten about.

'Sorry, I completely forgot, I'm in the middle of this TV series. Sorry.'

'I know, that's why we're going to have to record your story up there. I need to book a studio.'

'Sorry?'

'Alright, you don't have to keep apologising. Let's just organise a time and day.'

No, no, I wanted to tell her, that wasn't an 'apology sorry', it was a 'what the hell are you talking about sorry'.

'You haven't changed the title have you? It's still called *The Fib?*

Ah, now I know what she is on about.

'No, no, it's still called *The Fib*. I'm rather pleased with it.'

Talk about life reflecting art, here am I, telling whoppers. The title was all I had. I hadn't written a word. I'd completely forgotten that I had been commissioned to write it. Not a problem – once the TV series is out of the way I'll get on with it, shouldn't take me more than a couple of days, I'd got the story worked out ... more or less ....

'Good, because that's what's in the *Radio Times*. It's going out next Thursday by the way.'

Words cannot describe my reaction to this last remark. Incredulous, amazed, rooted to the spot – they don't come anywhere near. Expletive-omitted gobsmacked perhaps comes the closest.

'So we'll have to record it by the end of this week. Can you fax me a copy?'

118

A nano-second of horror turns to an oh-no-second of terror.

'Err ... fax you a copy ... it's ... err, handwritten, you'll never be able to read it.'

My problem is not that I have now got to work late into the next night or three to get this story written but that the plot – yes, I truly had worked it out ... more or less – the plot hinges on a real life-figure, and not just any old real-life figure but a living legend. A certain Bobby Charlton and without his permission there ain't gonna be no story.

So, I telephone Mr Charlton, as he then was, at Preston North End AFC and ask to speak to the Manager, as he then was, and explain my dilemma.

'... and *The Fib* is already listed in the *Radio Times* and if you don't give me permission ...'

Plee-ease, I'm saying to myself.

' ... you'll come across great in the story, a real hero, I promise you ... '

Permission was graciously given. Sir Bobby is a real hero. The story was written, recorded and broadcast the following Thursday.

Thanks Bobby.

GARY LINEKER

—◄○►—

Former England striker and captain, who played for Leicester City, Everton, Tottenham Hotspur, Barcelona and Grampus Eight during a spectacularly successful career. Now a BBC television sports presenter.

A Manchester City player was being interviewed on the radio before the start of the 2003/04 season, and was saying how much he was looking forward to it.

'We have every reason for optimism,' he said, 'because we have a very young squad. In fact,' he continued, proving that he spent more time on the football pitch as a lad than in the maths classroom, 'we are all roughly the same on average.'

Aren't we all?

JULIAN LLOYD WEBBER

Cellist and lifelong Leyton Orient fan.

Variations on a Team

Leyton Orient were responsible for my winning a gold disc for a recording within five weeks of its release.

I had wanted my brother Andrew to write a piece using the cello for several years, both because of his gift for writing tunes and because I felt he would approach the cello in a new and creative way. For a while he stalled on the idea, basically because he wasn't sure the cello could be made to work with rock instruments.

In the end the decision whether or not to go ahead rested on a bet between us on the outcome of Orient's final match of the 1976/77 season, against Hull City. There was a time when Andrew went to lots of Orient matches, but his patience had finally worn thin. That season the O's were in a not unfamiliar position – they had to get at least a draw in their final match to remain in the old Second Division. Andrew was not convinced they could even manage that, but I knew the lads would pull through.

The bet was that if Orient managed to draw, or even win, then Andrew would finally have to write the piece. In true Roy of the Rovers style, Orient battled to a nail-biting 1–1 draw, and so Variations was finally born.

M

MARTIN McCAGUE

<o>

*British-born but Australian-bred Kent and England fast
bowler, who played three Tests for England in the 1990s.*

When I was picked to tour Australia in 1994/95, I had
to endure months of taunting from the Australian people
about my electing to play for England. Towards the end
of the tour, we were invited to attend a dinner with the
then Prime Minister of Australia, Bob Hawke. I was somewhat surprised to hear him say that it was great that
Australia had had some input into the progress of my
career at Kent and England. I left the dinner feeling a lot
happier, but was quickly brought back down to earth
whilst queuing for a taxi back to the hotel. When I opened
the taxi door, the driver refused point blank to take me, on
the grounds that I was a 'traitor' and 'the rat who joined
the sinking ship'.

This was all a bit rich, considering that the taxi driver was
Croatian!

LIZ McCOLGAN

—◄◦►—

*Dundee-born Liz McColgan won a gold medal for
the 10,000 metres in the Commonwealth Games held
in Edinburgh (1986) and at the world championships in
Tokyo in 1991. She also won the London Marathon
in 1996, and a silver medal for the 10,000
metres in the Seoul Olympics (1988).*

One of the funniest things that a friend of mine said to me was, 'There's not much to this marathon running. It all seems pretty easy. All you have to do is sprint to the front and stay there, and don't let anyone pass you.'

That was someone who obviously knows nothing about running and racing.

IAN MCINTOSH

◄○►

Hugely successful coach of both Natal Sharks
and the Springboks rugby teams in the 1990s.

Frans Erasmus, the Springbok and Eastern Province prop, arrived late and exhausted at a shortened line-out called by the opposition. When Eastern Province were warned by the referee that they had one too many in the line-out, Frans replied, 'Ag, Mister Ref, if you let me stay here, I promise I won't do anything.'

Then there was Gerrard Harding, the former Natal Sharks Prop, who only had one eye. He was packing down in the scrum against Eastern Transvaal in a night game when suddenly the lights went out. The players were called off the field. Upon entering the tunnel he asked the coach what had happened.

'The lights went off,' replied the coach.

'Thank heavens for that,' said Gerrard. 'I thought I had lost my other eye.'

MICK McMANUS

◄○►

Back in the 1960s, 70s and 80s,
welterweight McManus was a household name,
the man that wrestling fans loved to hate. An extremely
convincing villain, he fought against all
the top good guys of the era.

I was presented to HRH Princess Anne at a charity function at the Grosvenor House Hotel, and she was reported as saying in one of the papers the following morning, 'I didn't recognise you with your clothes on.'

This wasn't quite true. What she actually said was, 'The public doesn't usually see you fully clothed.'

* * *

Lew Barnes, a professional wrestler with very little talent, badly wanted an engagement with Dale Martin Promotions, one of the major promoters of wrestling. He was speaking to Jack Dale, one of the directors and matchmaker of the company, and in order to get a booking suggested he receive no fee, just travelling expenses.

Jack made no response so Lew said, 'All right, all right, I'll wrestle for nothing – it won't cost you one penny.'

Jack thought for a moment, and then said, 'No, Lew, you are still too dear.'

AND TONIGHT, AS A SPECIAL TREAT...

CHRISTOPHER MARTIN-JENKINS

◄○►

*Distinguished cricket correspondent, mainly
for* The Daily Telegraph *and* The Times, *and also
a key member of BBC radio's* Test Match Special *team
for over 30 years. Father of Sussex all-rounder
Robin Martin-Jenkins.*

E.W. Swanton, long-time cricket correspondent of *The Daily Telegraph* in days when that paper's cricket coverage was second to none, was my journalistic mentor in the early days of my working life on *The Cricketer* magazine. He became a supportive friend thereafter. Jim, as everyone knew him, lived life much as he wanted to, rather than allow events to dictate to him. As a young man, therefore, he played more or less as much club cricket as he wished, scoring enough runs and making sufficient friends to play in two games for Middlesex against university opposition.

Notoriously inclined to pomposity, Jim was often the butt of jokes from those who felt strong enough to pull his leg. One such was the mischievously witty J.J. Warr, of Cambridge, Middlesex and England fame. He famously defended Jim against a charge of snobbery by pointing out that he was perfectly prepared to travel in the same car as his chauffeur.

He went on playing at least into his sixties, not least for the club he co-founded, the Arabs. His final game for them had an unfortunate beginning but it illustrated Jim's belief that the highest standards of decorum should be applied at all times, on and off the field.

The game, at Lord Kingsdown's private ground at Torrey Hill, involved some high-class club cricketers in all senses. Having taken his side into the field first, 'The Founder' as he was known to all the younger Arabs in his exclusive club, was appalled to see the first ball from his fast bowler lift off a length to strike the opposing opening batsman in the face.

The young player was wearing a striped cap, not, it need hardly be said, a helmet. It gave him no protection from such a vicious first ball and he fell to the ground at once, blood pouring from a wound near his mouth.

Taking immediate charge, Jim clicked his fingers and summoned his wife Ann, who was watching in the Swanton Jaguar from the edge of the outfield, to come onto the field at once with the first-aid kit. A fine sportswoman herself in her youth, Ann came tripping onto the greensward as fast as her high heels would allow. Reaching for a bandage, she leant towards the stricken batsman even as he groaned and managed to lift his head an inch or two from the turf.

'Oh, I'm awfully sorry,' said Jim at once. 'I don't think you've met my wife. Ann: this is ....'

CHRISTOPHER MATTHEW

◄○►

Best-selling author of books such as Now We Are Sixty, Now We Are Sixty And A Bit *and* The Crisp Report *among many others.*

Mid-afternoon on a typically Greek scorcher in September 1976, and I was fielding at deep square on the Corfu Cricket Ground. I had turned out for a Cricketer Magazine XI, led by the erstwhile Captain of Hampshire, Ben Brocklehurst. We were playing Byron – one of the two Corfiot cricket clubs, the other being Gymnastikos.

Thanks to some low, fast stuff from Byron's two strike bowlers, Condos and Costelletos, who toiled unchanged throughout the innings and produced unplayable balls which came off the coconut matting at angles that defied the laws of physics – we had been bowled out for a creditable 110.

I never saw a single ball that came my way, but somehow managed to score 2. M. Wingfield-Digby was top scorer with an exuberant 29.

The Byron innings began badly. Their opener, Spiros Anemogianos, a short, stout, jolly looking man in a battered trilby and huge moustache, ran himself out and – without pausing – into a local café, where he stayed for the next hour, his head in his hands, sobbing his heart out.

With the score at 9 for 4, and F.R. Brown's son bowling from the Royal Palace End, Costelletos came in, adopted an early nineteenth-century stance and was promptly caught behind off a thick edge by Wingfield-Digby. However, as far as he was concerned, the decision was far from cut and dried. He stood there defiantly, until someone enquired tentatively 'Ow 'dat?' at which the umpire shook his head and, with a contemptuous sneer, Costelletos resumed his stance.

The next ball was short, fast and lifting and caught Costelletos sharply on the back of the head. He threw down his bat and, clutching his head, marched off the field, hurling insults at each fielder as he passed.

A long pause ensued, during which we stood about in an uneasy group in the middle of the wicket, anticipating the imminent outbreak of hostilities.

It was at this point that Ben Brocklehurst approached me and explained, very quietly, that the aim was to make all matches against the Greeks appear as closely fought as possible, and would I mind 'twiddling the arm a bit'?

From that moment on, the legend that the Corfiots are unable to cope with slow bowling was destroyed once and for all when two dozen runs were scored off two overs of the slowest deliveries ever seen in the Eastern Mediterranean.

'Just what we needed,' murmured Ben as the ball streaked yet again towards the Venetian Fortress boundary.

Byron were finally all out for 90. But honour had been satisfied and everyone agreed it had been a perfectly respectable result. Spiros Anemogianos, grinning sheepishly, kissed each of us in turn, and we grinned back and assured him that the incident had long been forgotten. After all, it was only a game.

Or was it? Call me an old romantic, but to this day I still secretly think of myself as the man responsible for preventing the first Anglo-Corfiot war in history.

MICHAEL MELLUISH

—◄○►—

Former Cambridge University and Middlesex wicket-keeper who was understudy to the great J.T. Murray in the 1950s, and who went on to become President of MCC in 1991/92.

Swaranjit Singh, a fine off-cutter from India, who was an impressive sight in his beard and light-blue turban, was unexpectedly left out of the Cambridge side for the Varsity match in 1954. He was very disappointed, as his team-mates were. The last match of our tour was against Sussex at Horsham, and Swaranjit was twelfth man.

At tea, he was asked by our all-rounder, John Pretlove, to take the drinks order for close of play. It was very hot and John Langridge of Sussex was over 100 not out. About 6.15, Swaranjit set off to collect the drinks for eleven very thirsty players. Not knowing where to go, he started wandering round the ground. He was passing the tent of the Sussex President, Arthur Gilligan, who called him in.

'What will you have to drink, dear boy?' he asked, ever the thoughtful host.

'I'll have nine gin and tonics and two pints of beer,' Swaranjit replied. 'If that's all right.'

JUNE MENDOZA

————————◄○►————————

*Distinguished portrait painter who has
created portraits of most members of the Royal
Family (including the Prince of Wales three times), as
well as many others, from Joan Sutherland to Chris
Evert and Virginia Wade, not to mention the
House of Commons in session.*

I was with Alec and Eric Bedser in their wee cottage painting the background on my large double portrait of them. Because of a mild dose of food poisoning lunch was not exactly, to the concern of my hosts, on my agenda.

What on earth could they do for me? Inspiration! How about some home-grown rhubarb from our vegetable patch?

Perfect.

I now have a lasting fond memory of my two large gentlemen seated either side of me at their very small table in their tiny kitchen, concern replaced on their faces by beaming pleasure at having cared for me.

They watched every spoonful.

MURRAY MEXTED

<o>

One of the great All Blacks number 8s, who
played in 34 Tests in the 1980s. Now a successful
television sports commentator.

I guess the one piece of commentary that has caused the most discussion at this end of the world was my line at an All Black Test last year at Carisbrook, Dunedin, or 'The House of Pain', as the locals refer to it.

In the second minute of the Test match Aaron Mauger put a grubber kick through the Springbok back line and it bounced up perfectly for Rokocoko to gather and dive over in one sweet movement.

My description was, 'So slick, so smooth, almost a Brazilian ... in fact shades of Ronaldo!'

I'm not sure if you in the Northern Hemisphere understand what the term 'Brazilian' means. If you don't then I suggest you ask the closest young lady with a naughty smile!

VICKI MICHELLE

<o>

Comedy actress best known for her portrayal
of Yvette, the sexy French waitress, in the
long-running sitcom, 'Allo 'Allo.

One of my favourite sporting memories is when I ran for the first time at the Flora Fun Run, in 2003, on behalf of the Lady Taverners.

Everyone went off at a great pace except for Faith Brown, Rachael Heyhoe Flint and myself. Faith and I not being great joggers for two obvious reasons (especially Faith!), we decided to set off at a more genteel pace.

We jogged a little, we walked a lot, we bantered with the onlookers (especially the men!), and laughed all the way to the end. Wanting to get to the finish line before nightfall, my competitive spirit took over and I made Faith sprint the last leg with Rachael and myself.

We actually finished in a very good time and more importantly raised money for the Lady Taverners. Boy, did we ache the next day – and thanked our lucky stars Faith didn't end up with two black eyes!

ADRIAN MILLS

Actor and television presenter, associated for many years with the BBC TV programme That's Life.

I was asked to play for the opposition during a Lord's Taverners match at Arundel some years ago. Batting higher up the order than normal, as they thought I must be good if I played regularly for the Taverners, I decided to hook the bowler for four. The ball caught the top edge of the bat, hit me in the face and resulted in me being carried from the ground to the best applause I've ever had. It was a bad injury which needed fourteen stitches. I sat stunned in the dressing room while John Price ran to get his car to take me to hospital (seeing 'Sport' run was a shock in itself).

At that moment Chris Tarrant wandered in and said, 'I bet it was that bastard Robert Powell who did that to you.'

I said, 'Yes. Yes, how did you know he was the bowler?'

Tarrant replied, 'Well, I wasn't watching but I heard you scream, "Jesus Christ" as you fell, so it was obvious, really.'

HECTOR MONRO

Lord Monro of Langholm is a former
Conservative Minister for Sport (when he was
MP for Dumfries and Galloway) and President of
the Scottish Rugby Football Union.

Some pollsters were conducting a survey on health education in my constituency, knocking on doors in every street. One smart mahogany door was opened by an elderly colonel, looking a bit dishevelled.

'May we ask you a few questions about your health, please sir?' asked the pollster.

'Of course, my good fellow,' replied the colonel. 'Fire away.'

'Well,' said the pollster, 'the first question is: when did you last have sex with your wife?'

'1945,' said the colonel immediately.

'Goodness me. How did you recall that so quickly?'

The colonel looked at his watch. 'Well, it's only 20:15 now.'

PATRICK MOORE

Sir Patrick Moore CBE FRAS DSc, astronomer,
musician and broadcaster, is also a very keen cricketer.
He has played countless games for the Taverners, as
well as for and against villages across Sussex.

Near East Grinstead, 1946. I was just out of the RAF, and playing in a match between two local teams. I am a leg-spinner and no. 11 bat (my aim was always 100 wickets per season, which I achieved, and 100 runs, which I didn't).

I was in, 0 not out. The fast bowler bowled. Somehow I got my bat to it, and the ball went into the outfield, which was part of the farm ground. We ran. And ran. And ran. We ran 14 and then realised that the ball was immersed in a cowpat: the fielder for some reason was reluctant to delve in and get it out! My 14 stood and at the end I was 17 not out. My highest score of the season!

DIANA MORAN

*The 'Green Goddess' fitness expert
on BBC's* Breakfast Time *for
many years.*

I made my final and innocent piece to camera, as I wound up my early morning work-out, which was being held on the courts of the up-market Roehampton Tennis Club in London.

All participants, the majority of whom were men, were in a line holding onto the net – having been coerced by myself into doing deep knee bends – in time to music.

With a big smile, I proudly announced, 'Well, as you can see, it's not only balls that are bouncing on the courts this morning – it's members too!'

JOAN MORECAMBE

*Wife of the late Eric Morecambe,
and Founder President of
the Lady Taverners.*

Eric would sometimes drive down to Wiltshire to spend the day trout fishing. On one such occasion, having had little success on the riverbank, he decided that his chances would be greater if he sited himself on a patch of earth, which formed a small island just off the riverbank. With confidence, Eric made the short leap, but unfortunately his island consisted of a soft muddy and mucky mixture, into which he sank up to his waist.

I still remember my surprise that evening on seeing him stepping out of his car, wearing a blanket down to his ankles and carrying several items of clothing in a plastic bag. There cannot be many men who return home minus their underpants and with such a good excuse!

MARTYN MOXON

—◄○►—

Yorkshire and England opening batsman
whose top Test score was 99. He played ten
Tests for England in the late 1980s, and when he
retired at the end of 1997, he had scored over 21,000
runs and scored 45 centuries. Subsequently coach
at Yorkshire and Durham.

Peter Hacker of Notts was fielding in front of the Yorkshire fans during a one-day match. He was not having much luck and they were giving him a great deal of abuse. Then Graham Stevenson smashed the ball to him at long off, where he took a good catch. He immediately turned round towards the crowd to get some of his own back.

But unknown to poor Hacker, it was a no-ball and the batsmen were continuing to run. He could not hear his team shouting at him to return the ball as the noise from the crowd was far too loud. He just carried on bowing and otherwise gesticulating at the crowd, who of course were now giving him even more stick than before.

Hilarious scenes.

AL MURRAY

'The Pub Landlord' Perrier-award-winning comedian.
Also a graduate of Oxford University and the great-great-
great-great grandson of William Makepeace Thackeray.

Some – like the boy Wilkinson – are born to rugby, others aspire to rugby, and then there are those of us who have rugby thrust upon them. Having outgrown my strength (strength I am still waiting for to catch up) rugby and I were never destined to get along. It's the tackling you see. And the kicking. And the passing, but mainly the tackling. I don't like pain, least of all the pain that comes from trying to grab someone round their legs while they run away from you which could result in you being kicked in the face. Even this face wouldn't really benefit from being kicked, despite what the TV critic at *The Guardian* might think.

So when it came to a form match between iiJ and iiB, on which the pride of my classmates was hanging – so we were told – there was only going to be one outcome for this shivering, weedy centre, with cowardice as my shield and fear as my constant companion. We were losing, which was fine by me and frankly all of the rest of the pale brainy boys in my class, but Mr Boulting wasn't having it. I really liked Mr Boulting, he taught Latin very imaginatively and put on fun plays, but when he had his rugby head on he made no sense at all. As the game came to a close, iiB surged yet again for our try line and as Julian Rayner – whose voice had broken aged eleven and who used to cut a shockingly mature dash in the changing rooms – came powering towards us, I found myself on my own, the last redoubt, the sole defender, the last man standing. In other words I was going to have to tackle him (for tackling see above).

I gulped. Mr Boulting jumped up and down shouting at me to get Rayner.

'Tackle him, Murray, tackle him, go for his legs.'

And off I went, determined this time actually to tackle someone. I got close to Rayner, and he powered on. I got closer and realised I'd caught up with him. All very well, but now I had to bring Rayner down – and I couldn't. It was going to hurt, hurt like hell. So arms outstretched as if to tackle I ran close behind Rayner but couldn't make the moment happen, I let the pace slacken, and, as much as Mr Boulting hollered, Julian went over the try line, scored and iiB triumphed yet again.

I'm not proud of this incident, but I'm also glad I didn't get my teeth kicked in. This is also why I would like Sir Clive to know I am unavailable should he call.

N

DON NEELY

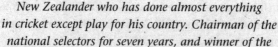

*New Zealander who has done almost everything
in cricket except play for his country. Chairman of the
national selectors for seven years, and winner of the
Plunket Shield as a player with Wellington. Also a
distinguished writer and historian of the game.*

I well remember a Test against the West Indies at the Basin
Reserve beginning on 20 February 1987. The West Indies
came into this, the first of three Tests, with the proud record
of having only been beaten four times in the 1980s and
having won five of their last seven Tests.

Upon winning the toss, Viv Richards exposed the New
Zealand batsmen to as accurate and fast attack as they have
ever faced – Marshall, Garner, Walsh and Holding. New
Zealand was saved by a tenacious innings of 75, made in 245
minutes by John Wright, playing in his 50th Test, as they
tottered to be all out for 228.

Greenidge and Haynes began with a century partnership
and New Zealand's total was overtaken for the loss of two

wickets. Facing a deficit of 117, the home team were 20 for 2 and their prospects as dismal as the conditions – cold, howling winds from the north that continually disturbed the bails – at the halfway mark of the game. Marshall showed a burst of pure violence, while Garner, Holding and Walsh lifted the ball threateningly. Occasionally the missile eluded the bat and the batsman was struck a concussive blow that floored him. Lying on the ground, vibrating like a tuning fork while the feeling of nausea spread throughout the body, Wright often found the bowling culprits sweating over him – adding insult to nauseating injury. But still he battled on.

Together with Martin Crowe, 241 runs were added to save the Test, with both batsmen scoring hundreds. Wright's innings was spread over three days and lasted 575 minutes. In his two innings he had occupied the crease for 828 minutes in scoring 75 and 137, enabling his team to achieve a memorable draw.

At the press conference afterwards, Wright apologised to those present for playing 'like an old spinster defending her honour'.

GARY NEWBON

◄◊►

In a long and distinguished career with ITV, Gary has covered seven World Cup finals and three European Championships for ITV, as well as three Olympic Games.

Sir Alf Ramsey's first match in charge of the England football team was a European Championship match against France in Paris on 27th February 1963. England lost 5–2.

Sir Alf, who liked to talk to players on an individual basis, said nothing until the end of the match. He sat down next to his captain, Jimmy Armfield, in the dressing room and said, 'Jimmy.'

'Yes, Alf,' replied Armfield.

'Do we always play like this?' asked Ramsey.

PAUL NIXON

Leicestershire and Kent wicket-keeper and batsman, who
has toured with England and England A without ever
winning a Test cap.

In 1998, with a couple of weeks left to the end of the season, we fixed a date for our end-of-season bash when we had a couple of days free, as it was the only time that all the guys and wives/girlfriends could be together, due to county players going abroad for the winter at the end of the season and so on.

As tends to happen after a few beers, a few party tricks came out. My party trick *used* to be to set my hands or clothes on fire using nail varnish remover.

Anyway, after two shandies, I was a little bit drunk, and when the party ended we went back to our captain, James Whittaker's place. At this point I decided to do my party piece, but, being slightly the worse for wear, I overloaded myself with about half a bottle of nail varnish remover instead of the usual capful!

I walked round the room with the lights off and my hands burning: everyone was very impressed. Unfortunately, I'd used so much nail varnish remover that I set the dining room table on fire (mind you, it should have been burnt years ago!) Everyone immediately tried to put the table fire out, and not my hands which were still burning and would not go out. They kept burning until eventually we doused the flames, but I was left with third degree burns – no skin left front or back.

This was just before two 'must win' games, which were two days later. I decided the story of my party trick had to be kept quiet from our manager, Jack Birkinshaw, as he would

That can't be why people say I remind them of a horse.

Sit down in front. I can't see.

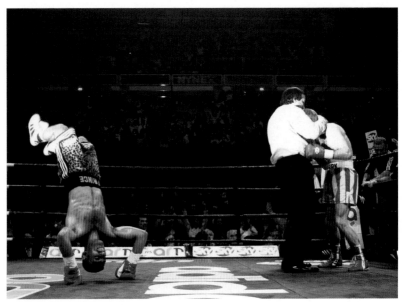

You can't disqualify me for hitting below the belt. He's standing on his head.

I hope there's a spare wheel in the boot.

I've found the putter. Pity about my caddy and the rest of the buggy.

RIGHT Thierry Henry –
always willing to give
a sample for the UEFA
testers, which Seaman
approved of whole-
heartedly.

BOTTOM LEFT
Synchronised ski-ing just
never caught on.

BOTTOM RIGHT
Mrs. Williams does
her best not to distract
attention from her
daughters.

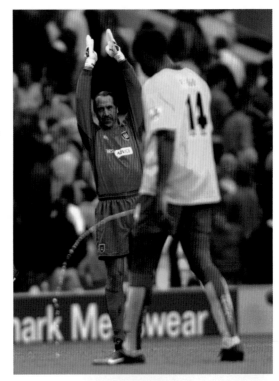

Disqualification was inevitable for using his arms in the early heats of the Olympic Riverdance competition.

The Germans have taken all the seats beside the pool, so I'm sunbathing here.

ABOVE What do you mean –
I was overacting?

RIGHT An English Rose topples
Nick Faldo. Unfortunately it's
not Justin.

Merde!

If I could just get on the ski-lift, I know I could be a contender.

Come back with my horse!

Brazil! It's just like watching Brazzz…

have gone crazy. So no one told him. During the matches I used little strips of artificial fat tissue on the front and back of my hands. This is normally used in burns units, but I didn't go to the hospital. During the matches, every time I had to catch the ball I was in the most pain I have ever been in, in my life – I asked the captain to put the spinners on after the first over, but even though he sometimes listened to my advice, this time he didn't!

We eventually told the manager after the last game at The Oval when the champagne was flowing and Leicester had won the County Championship.

O

NICK OWEN

*Sports broadcaster, writer and
presenter who has written several books
about sports oddities and disasters. For
many years he was the co-presenter of a
BBC daytime television show with
Anne Diamond, which set the standard
for all others to emulate.*

A golfer was unable to concentrate on his golf because
he suffered from terrible headaches. A friend said he had
had the same problem, and he used to go back home to his
wife and lay his head between her breasts for a couple of
hours.

'It's so relaxing, and I always feel better afterwards. You
should try it yourself.'

So the golfer tried it, and the headaches disappeared.
His golf improved and all was well in his world. The
next time he saw his friend, he thanked him for his
advice.

'It really worked,' said the golfer. 'And by the way, you've got a lovely house!'

P

CECIL PARKINSON

<o>

*Rt Hon Lord Parkinson of Carnforth was Conservative
Member of Parliament, and a cabinet minister (Trade
and Industry, Transport etc.) for many years under
Margaret Thatcher and John Major.*

My first job after leaving Cambridge was as a management
trainee with the Metal Box Company. My first major assignment was to spend eight months at a huge Metal Box factory
in Neath in South Wales, where rugby union was a religion
rather than a mere sport.

On our first Saturday, we went to watch Neath play
Aberavon, having had a pint of beer or two to prepare
ourselves for the match. Neath had a most impressive
bald-headed man playing on the left wing. He was amaz-
ingly resilient and seemed to bounce back whenever
Aberavon tackled him. We were standing on the Terrace
and I was standing next to a very large Welshman, a keen
Neath supporter. At half-time, I turned to him and said,
'Who is the bald-headed old bugger on the wing?' to which

this huge man replied, 'He is my brother, Cyril, and he is 24.'

I immediately went on to say what a splendid winger he was, in spite of having no hair, and of course you could tell he wasn't very old!

THESE ARE HIS OTHER BROTHERS AND THAT'S OUR MAM!

NICHOLAS PARSONS

◄○►

Broadcaster and entertainer extraordinary, Nicholas Parsons first came to the public's attention on The Arthur Haynes Show *in the 1950s. He has presented the BBC radio comedy quiz* Just A Minute *for over 30 years. He was President of the Lord's Taverners in 1998 and 1999.*

As a member of the Lord's Taverners, I have turned out for them in a large number of charity matches over a period of 40 years. In my youth I could put in a reasonable performance, but as you grow older, and with no match practice, every game becomes a challenge. For this reason, in a charity game I would always rather bat against a professional bowler than a keen club cricketer. The latter, who probably plays in front of a handful of spectators at club events, is often extremely keen to get you out, and then presumably boast later to his friends about all the celebrity scalps he has taken. An experienced professional bowler is going to be much more easy-going. He knows that if he puts his mind to it, he could probably bowl you out four balls out of six. He also has the skill to place the ball fairly gently outside the off-stump so that if you have any ability at all, you can score runs off him.

I had the perfect example of this in a Taverners match in 1990. We were playing Gestetner, who were sponsoring the game, and their managing director, who was an Australian, had reinforced his side by inviting a friend of his, Dennis Lillee, to turn out for them.

In our charity games, every celebrity who can put his arm over is usually asked to bowl a couple of overs, as the spectators like to see them in action. I was captain for the game, so I put myself on to bowl quite late in the innings. In my first over, Dennis Lillee was still batting. I am capable of bowling one or perhaps two good balls a season. One of these went to Dennis Lillee, and whether it was surprise on his part or a sudden mental blackout I will never know. I bowled him middle stump. With the spectators' applause resounding in my ears, it would have been marvellous to have retired gracefully from the sport at that moment, especially in view of what happened next.

Dennis Lillee was followed to the crease by the captain of the Gestetner team, the man who had underwritten £5,000 to the charity. The next ball I bowled turned out to be the other good ball I bowl in a season, and I claimed his wicket as well, caught behind. I had done the unforgivable. I had dismissed not only their captain but also the man responsible for their sponsorship, first ball. I turned to the umpire and suggested that he should rule it was a bump ball and call the batsman back, but he was not an umpire conversant with the ground rules of charity cricket, and he informed me that the batsman was out. My elation turned to embarrassment; I wished to retire from the sport for an entirely different reason.

Later, when I went out to bat, Dennis Lillee was bowling. The crowd thought they would see a few sparks fly. I was a little anxious myself, but in the tradition of true sportsmanship and fair play that exists among professional cricketers he bowled me a gentle one, which I was able to strike for four. I even took another boundary off him, and then he decided that I had had enough fun at his expense, and sent a ball down that bowled me all ends up. Two fours off Dennis Lillee, however, became another reason why I wished to retire gracefully from the sport after this particular game.

MIN PATEL

◄○►

*Kent and England left-arm spinner, who
but for injury would no doubt have played
for England much more often.*

You would think Michael Holding would know his way around the UK, having spent numerous summers on the county circuit with Derbyshire, then later as a television pundit. But when he was commentating on the fourth West Indies v England Test at Old Trafford in 1995, he was still somewhat unsure how to negotiate the approximately two-mile drive from the Copthorne Hotel in Salford Quays to the ground. Then Mikey had a moment of pure genius!! He would follow one of the England team (who were also in residence there) to the ground. Spotting a certain G.A. Hick heading out of the front doors, Michael sped to his car.

It was about an hour later, while heading South down the

M6 at a fair lick, that it dawned on the Windies speedster that Hick had been left out of the final eleven and was heading home to Worcester!

MARY PETERS

Dame Mary won the gold medal for the pentathlon at the 1972 Olympics in Munich, and has since devoted most of her time to furthering the cause of sport for all in Northern Ireland.

Fame is a strange thing. A grandmother wrote to me that her granddaughter had written in her school essay that she loved to train at the Saint Mary Peters track! Then a man stopped me in Prague to tell me that he had named his greyhound after me, adding, 'And she's a great bitch!'

My autobiography was called *Mary P.* I was told that if I wrote a sequel, I could call it 'Mary P's Again'!

GENE PITNEY

Legendary American singer, originator of '24 Hours From Tulsa' and 'Something's Gotten Hold Of My Heart', and the writer of 'He's A Rebel', 'Rubber Ball' and 'Hello Mary Lou'.

My Tough Year in Baseball

When I was about seven years old I was really into baseball. The big thing was Little League Baseball and I just had to give it a try. I played sand lot ball with my friends in the neighbourhood but had never attempted organised sport. I went along to the tryouts and, along with many others, ran, hit, pitched, all the things you do to play baseball. When it came time to pick the team I was not selected.

Not to be deterred I stayed and tried out for what was called the Farm Team – no idea why! This was the second-string team of players not good enough to make the first team. I was heartbroken when I was turned down for this as well. It was a long trek up the three hills to my home. Thinking back I realise now that, as mothers do, my mother felt worse than I did about my experience!

This may have been the start of what sent me on a more unique form of athletic endeavours. My future successful sports would include ice-skating, swimming, running, hunting, fishing, and trapping. Luckily, I sang while pursuing all of the above!

PETER POLYCARPOU

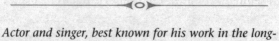

Actor and singer, best known for his work in the long-running BBC TV sitcom Birds Of A Feather, *and in the National Theatre's hit production of* Oklahoma.

I was captain of my school cricket side in 1975, and for a Cypriot this was unusual in itself. I mean how many other Cypriot captains of cricket do you know? Graham Able, who is now master at Dulwich College and a personal friend, had asked me to lead the side in my last term at school. We had had a brilliant season and were in Cricket Week, that glorious time after term is over when you play a match every day and don't do anything else. No exams, no teachers, no rules and the village pub isn't out of bounds!

It was the game against the local village side of Sutton Valence and I had won the toss and decided to bat. I usually went in at number three but we were going so well that I hadn't been needed before lunch. Even after lunch my openers, David Foster and Mark Benson, were going very well and never looked like they were in trouble. (Mark later went on to captain Kent for many years and also played for England.) He had got a century and I was going to wait for David to get his before declaring. He was going well but just couldn't get past his nervous nineties. To make matters worse the headmaster had had a quiet word in my ear along the lines of 'You can't leave it too long or you won't have time to get them out.' As each over passed I had less and less time to bowl them out.

After what seemed like an age I took the decision to declare and by that time David had reached 98 not out! He was furious and threw his bat down in the middle, making me and everybody else know how angry he was. I apologised and tried to explain that we were dangerously short of time and had to get out there and bowl. He managed to compose himself enough to be the first change bowler for me, as my opening pace bowlers hadn't managed to take a wicket and the village side were piling on the runs.

David Foster was also a very good left-arm spinner who came around the wicket. All season he had been at the top of the averages or thereabouts. He took the first wicket for me, and as I captained from behind the stumps I could see he was on fire and practically unplayable that day. He took a second and a third in consecutive overs. When he got his fifth it was a momentous day for him. He then proceeded to get a sixth and a seventh wicket so I just let him carry on bowling all day. David ended up with all ten wickets and we presented him with the match ball. I think we carried him off on our shoulders.

He has never forgiven me, however, for declaring when he was on 98 not out! Who'd be a captain eh?

KIERAN PRENDIVILLE

──────◄○►──────

A television presenter and a reporter in science, news and sport, yet he is probably best known for his work as a creator and writer of popular drama, with hits such as Badger, Roughnecks, *and* Ballykissangel.

OUR MAN AT WATERSHEDDINGS

Many years ago, I worked as a sports reporter for an Oldham news agency, covering the local football and rugby league clubs. Amongst many discerning clients, our stuff was carried by the Saturday edition of the *Manchester Evening News*, the football pink. This meant that every ten minutes throughout the match, the phone would ring in the press box and a copytaker would expect two hundred sparkling words off the reel.

One Saturday in the late 60s, Oldham Rugby League Club played Wigan. Happily for me, I was covering Oldham Athletic v Plymouth Argyle down the road. I remember this particularly because an embittered tea girl had got the club disc jockey to play 'Hey Big Spender' over the Boundary Park public address system, and dedicate it to me to mark our date the week before. But that's not the point of the story.

The real story was happening up the road at Watersheddings where a colleague – who has begged me to protect his anonymity (no problem Geoff) – was covering the rugby. He'd never covered rugby before. What I know now but didn't know then is that he'd never sat through a game in his life. But just like actors who falsely claim horse riding, fencing and fifteen language skills on their cv, so he had invented an affinity with the working man's game to get the gig.

157

Aware of his limitations, he studied hard for the big one. He did a good job too. Every ten minutes the phone rang and Geoff wasn't found lacking. Eagerly he took his chance. His words twinkled and danced. Reading his copy later, you felt every tackle, scored every try. You felt you were there. By the end of the match, 800 words later, Geoff was feeling pretty pleased with himself. Confident too. So confident, he suggested to a grizzled old season ticket holder that Oldham had performed pretty well under the circumstances.

As Oldham had in fact been walloped by a cricket score, this went down like a cup of cold tea. As the fan set him straight, a chill ran through Geoff's bones. He had attributed every score to the wrong player in the wrong team. And every golden word was now, literally, set in stone.

This led to the most embarrassing correction ever dictated by a sports hack. Wisely eschewing direct contact with the sports desk, Geoff asked to speak to Vera, the same copytaker who had typed out his match report.

'I've got an addition to my match report.'

'Don't be daft, Geoff, we're going to press.'

'It's really important.'

'Is there much?'

'Not really.'

'Where does it go?'

'Right after the final score.'

'Go on then.'

'For Oldham read Wigan, for Wigan read Oldham.'

DAVID PURDIE

Professor, surgeon, gynaecologist and expert on osteoporosis. Also a very funny after-dinner speaker.

Psychological warfare is officially frowned upon, but is in full – and often none too subtle – operation across the nation's golf courses.

Some years ago, playing foursomes for Scottish Universities Old Boys against the (formidable) undergraduate Golf Team of St Andrews, I was partnered by the splendid Ian Simpson QC – now a learned Judge. At one hole I drove off, followed by the student. His drive was hit wildly out to the right and flashed away over a bank of whins, behind which another foursome was approaching – and we all heard a sickening smack! This was actually the ball hitting a whin stem flush-on , but none of us back on the tee knew this.

It was too good to miss. I said to the student, who was now distinctly pale, 'Sorry, but it's my professional opinion that that was the sound of a ball impacting in a human head. But don't worry. It's by no means always fatal.'

The student said to his partner, 'Oh God. Take my clubs. I must go and see what's happened.'

As he made to run off the tee, Ian gently restrained him.

'Before you go,' said he in his best barrister's baritone, 'I have to say that it's my professional opinion – which will cost you nothing – that the way you rolled your wrists on your backswing could be construed in Court as negligent.'

We won the next three holes.

Q

TREVOR QUIRK

—◄○►—

South African wicket-keeper batsman who is now the
leading television sports commentator in his country,
and a legend to all those who have heard him at work.

Before I became a full-time sports broadcaster, commentating mostly on cricket and golf, I played first-class cricket for Northern Transvaal from 1971 to 1979. My debut was a Currie Cup match against Rhodesia, now Zimbabwe, which in those days played in all South Africa's domestic competitions.

We won the toss and our captain, Jackie Botten, who opened the bowling for the Springboks in England in 1965, elected to bat. Michael John Proctor, who played a couple of seasons for Rhodesia before returning to Natal, opened the bowling and with his first ball uprooted our opening batsman's off-stump. It might have been a good thing for me in a way not to have to sit anxiously waiting for my debut innings. So in I went, a youngster totally unprepared for the greeting I was to receive out in the middle.

While I was taking guard Ray Gripper, the Rhodesian captain, fielding at forward short leg, asked Springbok leg-spinner, Jackie du Preez, fielding at backward short leg, 'Who is this lighty?'

'I think he's some little wanker called Quirk,' said du Preez.

'Why are his legs shaking?' asked Gripper, and they both started sniggering. My legs had not been trembling, but when I looked up and saw Proccie waiting to tear in from the sight screen they started shaking uncontrollably. Inevitably the first ball was one of those bouncers that when you try and sway out of the way just keep following you. No helmets in those days, so it rearranged the cap on my head and down I went on my backside.

As I clumsily got up, much to the mirth of all around me, I looked up to see Proccie standing a yard away.

'Oopsy daisy boytjie,' he said. 'The next one will take your effing head off.'

That was my welcome to Currie Cup cricket.

R

CLIVE RADLEY

—◆—

*Middlesex and England batsman, who
played eight Tests for England in the late
1970s. He hit two Test hundreds, and finished
with an average of 48.10. In a career stretching
from 1964 to 1987, he hit over 26,000
runs and 46 centuries.*

A local derby – Middlesex v Surrey at Lord's. Pat Pocock arrived at the crease to bat wearing spectacles, which nobody had seen him wearing before.

Fred Titmus, the bowler, politely enquired, 'What have you got those things on the end of your nose for, Perce?' (Pocock was known throughout cricket as 'Percy' for some reason.)

'They are because I'm bloody deaf. Why do you think?'

Titmus then bowled Pocock with his first delivery. As the dejected batsman walked past him back to the pavilion, Titmus remarked, 'You didn't hear that one too well, though, did you?'

CHRIS REA

Head of Communications at the International Rugby Board, Chris Rea began his career as a commentator on televised rugby matches, and became a key part of ITV's rugby commentary team.

The Rugby World Cup in South Africa, 1995. As part of the ITV commentary team, I was down to commentate on the match between Scotland and Tonga with my co-commentator, the late Gordon Brown – Broon frae Troon. In the Tongan team was a tight-head prop exotically, and from a commentator's point of view dangerously, named Fuko Fuka.

Ten minutes into the match, and Fuko Fuka fells the Scottish captain Gavin Hastings. Turning to Broon, I said, 'The Tongan tight-head prop – a little indiscreet with his boot, wouldn't you say, Gordon?'

'Yes,' came the reply. 'Silly Fuka.'

TIM RICE

——◄◊►——

*Sir Tim is an Oscar- and Grammy-winning
lyricist, broadcaster and cricket enthusiast who
was president of MCC in 2003, and of the Lord's
Taverners from 1988 to 1990, and in 2000.*

Some bat, some bowl, some field. I attempt all these things
when playing cricket but there is one vital area of the game
in which I have few peers – captaincy, or leadership as I
prefer to think of it. Heartaches CC are a tricky bunch to
control and I need all my people skills to keep the side
focused on the goal of victory. It is only through my efforts
that a disparate collection of self-centred individuals are
welded together as a team, and that only after an enormous
struggle to get them to the ground in the first place. Few of
my fellow sporting leaders face the challenges I do week in
week out every summer. Does Michael Vaughan ever receive
a phone call from Marcus Trescothick on the morning of a
Test match informing him that he can't play as he has to
take the kids to see their grandmother? Does Freddie Flintoff
ever cry off at the last minute because he met, and is still
with, someone particularly interesting at a party last night?
Does his pace attack ever miss the first thirty minutes of a
game because the directions to Trent Bridge weren't clear?
Exactly.

I put up with all of this and more, which is why I
treasure every example of respect shown to me by my
players. Against Williamstrip, deep in the Cotswold country-
side, a few years back, I had astutely identified the wicket
as one likely to help my left-arm floaters, assuming they
ever got the chance to land on the pitch before they reached
the batsman. My lengthy spell was not quite going as

planned and I detected rumbles of resentment, even muttered hints that a bowling change would not come amiss, from more than a couple of fielders. Thus I was very touched to be told by veteran wicket-keeper Harold Caplan that I should 'keep bowling until the cows come home'.

With this endorsement from a senior professional ringing in my ears, I confidently turned around to start another over, only to be confronted with – a herd of cows, wandering across the adjacent field, clearly coming home. Harold has since responded to public demand and retired to take up umpirical duties for Heartaches, where he is doing even more damage to the cause than he did as a stumper. I am still leader.

WENDY RICHARD

—◄○►—

Actress whose career has spanned roles from the ditzy Miss Brahms in Are You Being Served? *to the everlastingly unfortunate Pauline Fowler in* EastEnders. *She also has a number one hit single to her credit: in 1961 she duetted with Mike Sarne on a comedy hit called* Come Outside.

I used to be pally with the late great Denis Compton and we would often meet for a glass of medicine together. On one occasion I looked through the pub window and saw two mounted policemen, one of whom was putting a ticket on Denis' car.

I rushed out, followed by Denis, and said, 'How dare you put a ticket on that car! Do you not know who this gentleman is?'

The policeman said, 'No ma'am, but I know who you are.'

I said, 'Never mind about me. This gentleman is Denis Compton. He is our country's greatest living sportsman, who has played cricket for his country at Lord's and football for Arsenal.'

Whereupon the officer got off his horse, removed the ticket and rode off into the sunset.

DAVID RIPLEY

◄○►

Northamptonshire CCC wicket-keeper/batsman from 1984 to 2001. He scored 8,693 runs in his career, including nine centuries, and dismissed 763 batsmen.

In the Northants v Essex match in 1999, in which David Sales hit 303 not out to become the youngest ever English triple centurion, the Essex wicket-keeper Barry Hyam was on a pair. He'd made a duck in the first innings, and at tea he was 0 not out in his second innings. On resumption after tea, we discovered that a pear had been mysteriously placed on the wicket for Barry to see. In the first over after tea, bowled by Graeme Swann, the prime suspect in the pear placement, Barry was bowled, thus completing his pair.

* * *

Curtly Ambrose, the great West Indian fast bowler who played for several seasons for Northants, decided to go out one evening. I asked him where he was going, and he said, 'To Milton Keynes.'

'To see friends? To go to the movies? To have a meal?' I enquired.

The most feared fast bowler in the world looked at me and said, 'To play bingo.'

JOHN ROBBIE

—◄◦►—

Former Ireland and British Lions rugby player who has become a major radio star in South Africa, hosting the most important breakfast news show in the country.

People don't believe me when this story is told.

In 1980, in Port Elizabeth in the dressing room just before the deciding Test of the Springboks versus British Lions series, Tony Ward discovered he had forgotten his boots. I was changing beside him and he told only me. We were the half back reserves and he was also the reserve goal kicker. It was a dreadful day, with rain and sleet sheeting down, and the roads were chaos. We got to the ground late and all was panic and rush. Tony possesses the tiny feet of a ballet dancer and nobody else's boots fitted. Fearing an almighty row, I told him to stay quiet and not to tell anyone. Remember subs only came on due to injury in those days. We'd be okay I told him, trying to sound confident. If we kept quiet.

Due to the crowd pressing back to get under the grandstand roof, we subs couldn't get out to the area in which we were due to sit, and instead had to exit at the rear of the stand and walk around and then over the terraces to gain access from the front. When I close my eyes I can still see his little feet squelching through the puddles. As we walked we heard the roar as the players ran on and the game started. As we came over the terraces, through the gloom we

169

saw there was an early stoppage. Ollie Campbell, the Lions fly half, was on the ground with blood pumping from his head. Coach Noel Murphy turned back and called for Wardie to go on. Tony looked at the packed stadium, then at his damp stockinged feet and then at me. His eyes were wide with terror.

'What do I do now?' he hissed, as though it was all my fault. I answered, 'Now you pray.'

The prayers were answered as Ollie played on, and to this day Noel Murphy and the rest of the Lions management still don't know that in what was then the decider in a series for the unofficial rugby championship of the world, their reserve fly half and ace kicker nearly had to take the field in his stockinged feet.

I can't imagine it happening today.

TIM ROBINSON

—◆◇◆—

Nottinghamshire and England opening batsman, who played 29 Tests, hitting four centuries, between 1984 and 1989. In first-class cricket, he scored over 27,000 runs and hit 63 hundreds.

Bruce, an Australian, landed at Heathrow to watch the Aussies in the Ashes series, and not feeling too well went to see the doctor.

'Hey doc, I don't feel too good,' said Bruce.

The doctor gave him a thorough check-up and informed Bruce he had prostate problems and the only cure was an immediate testicular removal.

'No way doc! I'm here for the Test series and I'm getting a second opinion!' said Bruce.

The second English doctor gave Bruce the same diagnosis, and said that testicular removal was the only cure. Bruce refused the treatment.

Bruce was devastated but on the morning of the first Test he found an Aussie doctor and decided to get one last opinion.

The diagnosis was the same, 'You've got prostate sickness mate!'

'What's the cure then doc mate?' asked Bruce, hoping for a different answer.

'Well,' said the doc, 'we're going to have to cut off your balls.'

'Phew, thank God for that,' said Bruce. 'Those pommy bastards wanted to take my Test tickets off me!'

BOBBY ROBSON

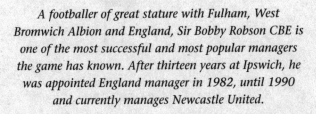

A footballer of great stature with Fulham, West Bromwich Albion and England, Sir Bobby Robson CBE is one of the most successful and most popular managers the game has known. After thirteen years at Ipswich, he was appointed England manager in 1982, until 1990 and currently manages Newcastle United.

Leicester City v Ipswich Town, Filbert Street, Leicester, 19th January 1974. At half-time, Leicester City were beating us 2–0. My chairman, John Cobbold, turned to me and said he thought Ipswich were playing some enlightening football, and had I done something special in training?

I realised my chairman thought we were winning. I turned to him and said, 'Leicester are playing in blue. We are the away team. We are in yellow and actually, Mr Chairman, we are losing 2–0.'

I cannot repeat his next statement. Leicester added three more goals in the second half, and we lost 5–0.

STRUAN RODGER

<>

Well-known actor whose television credits
include Rumpole Of The Bailey, Prime Suspect
and Poirot. *Leg-spin bowler and roll-your-*
own chain-smoker at mid-on.

Bobby Keetch and Johnny Haynes, both Fulham players, were great mates. The time came for the new round of wage negotiations with the club. Johnny Haynes went in to see the manager first.

When he came out, Bobby Keetch asked him how he had got on.

'They've offered me £100 a week during the season, and £70 a week in the summer.'

Keetch was impressed that the great Johnny Haynes had thus become the first British player ever to earn as much as £100 a week, and he went into his meeting with the manager with renewed confidence about the club's generosity.

'I'll offer you £80 a week during the season, and £50 a week in the summer,' the manager told him.

'No, you're not on,' said Bobby. 'You offered Haynes £100 a week, and £70 in the summer.'

'But Johnny's an international, a great player, and to be frank, a better player than you are.'

'Not in the effing summer, he isn't.'

BUDGE ROGERS

◄○►

One of the greats of English rugby, he played 34
internationals as a wing forward for England between
1961 and 1969, making him then the most capped
English player. He captained his club, Bedford, as well
as England and the Lions, and went on to become a
national coach and selector. For many years a
Trustee of the Lord's Taverners.

I was speaking at a small Welsh club dinner, and made the mistake of asking for questions. A small chap at the back stood up and said, 'Can you tell me, Mr Rogers, who scored the winning try against the 1906 All Blacks in the top right-hand corner of Cardiff Arms Park?'

I thought for a while for effect, and then said, 'I don't know. Can you tell me?'

He went up onto his toes and said, 'F***ing me!'

* * *

This is a story told by the late Jock Wemyss, who played for Scotland before and after the First World War, and who lost an eye in the war.

He was playing against France after the war. Jock had lost his right eye and his opposite number on the French side had lost his left eye. At the back of the line-out, they had to keep touching each other, so the referee came back to see what was going on. They told him, 'We have to check that the other guy is still there.'

ADRIAN ROLLINS

Batsman and wicket-keeper who played
for Derbyshire from 1992 to 1999, and for
Northamptonshire from 2000 to 2002.

Somerset v Derbyshire at Taunton, 1994, our last away game of the season. I was sleeping happily in my room, while my room-mate Peter Bowler was in the bar. I heard the door open, and presumed it was Pete. Next minute, WHOOSH! I was drenched in water. I staggered out of bed as quickly as I could and chased the perpetrators out of the room. I did not see them, but I thought I heard the laughter of Dominic Cork. I had no clothes on, so I went back to my room to get dried and dressed. Five minutes later, Phil DeFreitas and Chris Adams turned up, but claimed they had seen nothing.

In 1999, five years later, in my final season at Derby, I found out it was Adams, who by then had moved to Sussex, along with Cork and DeFreitas. Revenge is a dish best served cold. 2004 is my year for that revenge, so watch out.

Incidentally, the match, like my bed, was completely washed out, with only a few overs possible on the final afternoon.

JOSEPH ROMANOS

Leading New Zealand sports writer and
journalist, author of the official biography of
New Zealand's greatest post-war captain,
John Reid, and many other books.

Gary Bartlett is regarded as the fastest bowler in New Zealand cricket history, faster even than the young Richard Hadlee and Shane Bond.

Bartlett was really something when he burst into first-class and Test cricket as a teenager. He had even class batsmen like Australians Bobby Simpson and Ian Craig looking tentative and gave New Zealand real firepower. Not so much mention is made of his batting, but he wielded the bat usefully throughout his 11-year first-class career. He played one innings that deserves particular mention. It happened during the 1959–60 season, only his second in first-class cricket.

In Central Districts' match against Auckland that season, Bartlett batted really well and seemed set for his maiden first-class century. He and Central Districts captain Ian Colquhoun had added 133 in 99 minutes for the tenth wicket when Bartlett, on 99, pushed the ball away and called for the run that would give him his century. It was a comfortable enough single and it is easy to imagine how ecstatic the young Bartlett felt as he scurried through to reach the magic three figures.

Unbeknown to him, though, there was all sorts of drama happening behind his back. Colquhoun responded to the call quickly enough, but never did get to the other end. Halfway down the pitch, he tore a leg muscle and crumpled on the wicket in agony. He attempted to cover the remaining metres in a sort of crawl, but never made it. Colquhoun was run out and Bartlett was left stranded on 99 not out. He never did make a first-class century.

GRAHAM ROSE

—◄○►—

Middlesex and Somerset all-rounder, a key
member of Somerset's side throughout the 1990s.
He retired at the end of 2002 with a batting
average higher than his bowling average,
the mark of a true all-rounder.

The great Tommy Cooper was lining up to meet the Royal party after a Royal Variety Command Performance.

Eventually, he met the Duke of Edinburgh and they chatted about the forthcoming FA Cup Final, where the Duke was to present the Cup to the winners. Tommy asked the Duke if he was particularly interested in football.

When the Duke replied that he wasn't, Tommy asked, 'Well, can I have your tickets?'

* * *

I was batting at Taunton one day, preparing to take strike with the one and only Dickie Bird umpiring at the bowler's end. As the bowler started his run-up, the great man was rummaging in his pockets and a glazed look of horror came over his face.

He started wandering towards extra-cover, where he had been standing moments earlier, mumbling and moaning, 'It's no good, stop the game, stop the game!'

He was intently searching the floor, looking for something

vital. The bowler stopped his run-up and I asked, 'What's the matter, Dickie?'

He replied, somewhat distraught, 'I've lost one of me marbles!'

We all know that he lost those years ago!

GERALLT ROSSER

—◄○►—

Half of the music and comedy duo Rosser and Davies, fanatical rugby and golf fans and stalwarts of the Taverners after-dinner circuit.

After Wales' disastrous World Cup campaign in South Africa, when Wales failed to reach the quarter-final stages, Mike Hall, the Welsh captain, was walking through Cardiff city centre when he was approached by a fan.

'Excuse me,' he said. 'Sorry to bother you, but aren't you Mike Hall?'

'Yes, I am,' replied Mike, rather pleased to be recognised.

'Mike Hall, captain of the Welsh rugby team …?'

'That's right.'

'I hope you don't mind me asking,' continued the fan, 'but do you know Ieuan Evans by any chance?'

'Yes,' said Mike, slightly taken aback.

'Let me get this straight. You actually know Ieuan Evans?'

'Of course I do. I'm captain of the Welsh rugby team, out-side centre. I stand next to him.'

'That's incredible! You actually know Ieuan Evans, the greatest wing in world rugby, Wales' record try scorer, hero of the British Lions …'

'For the last time,' said Mike, beginning to get a bit exasperated. 'Yes, I know Ieuan Evans.'

'Well then,' said the fan, 'pass him the bloody ball.'

ROB ROTH

<o>

*American theatrical director, his credits including
the hit musicals* Aida *and* Beauty And The Beast.

While I was in high school, I never played, much less attended, any sporting event.

A good friend of mine was the captain of the wrestling team, and he came from a troubled home. His parents, for whatever reason, never would attend the wrestling matches to watch their son fight. I knew that this upset him, and so when he asked me to attend a match, I agreed.

The match was held in my high school gym, never one of my favourite rooms! My friend starts his bout. Suddenly he gets a very serious nosebleed – I mean there was blood all over the mat.

The referee didn't stop the match. I was very upset, and actually started crying. Eventually, my friend was pinned and the bout ended, but not before I was totally in tears. Happily a female gym teacher friend of mine brought me into her office and let me smoke a cigarette to calm down.

That was my first and last high school sporting event.

S

BROUGH SCOTT

*Racing commentator and writer,
presenter of Channel Four's racing
coverage for many years.*

Some years ago the Jockey Club made the extremely daring move of inviting the press to dinner in their marvellously traditional rooms at Newmarket – complete with a striped trousered butler straight out of P.G. Wodehouse.

'The Chablis or the claret, my lord,' asked Jeeves of the Senior Steward, before moving on to the long-haired, dodgy-suited hack in the next chair.

Jeeves summed up the situation with one long, utterly contemptuous look, before asking 'Red or White?'

DAVID SHEEPSHANKS

Chairman of Ipswich Town FC (but not the chairman referred to in Sir Bobby Robson's anecdote).

Johnny Cobbold, former long-serving Chairman of Ipswich Town Football Club, was a gentleman who did not tolerate stale and rather pompous people easily.

After a game at Portman Road against a Northern club he introduced himself to a certain titled director of the opposition.

He asked him if he would like a drink and the reply was, 'No drink has every passed my lips.'

The Town Chairman then said, 'Can I offer you a cigar?'

Back came the answer, 'I've never smoked in my life.'

Johnny then blurted out, 'In that case, we have nothing in common ... good day.'

DAVID SHEPPARD

————◄○►————

*The Rt Revd Lord Sheppard of Liverpool was
captain of Sussex and England, and is still the only
ordained priest to score a Test century. He then went on
to become Bishop of Liverpool and a leading social
reformer within the Church of England. Oddly,
he never played a Test at Lord's.*

My first match for Sussex was played against Leicestershire. I was eighteen, having just left school. I was warned about Jack Walsh. He bowled one left-hander's googly that he showed you, and one you couldn't read. Then they warned me about Willie Watson in the field, as he could throw with either hand. I promised I would look out for them. But the only ball I received in the first innings was from Vic Jackson!

In the second innings at the tea interval I was 0 not out. As we went out onto the field, the Leicester captain, Les Berry, fell back beside me and said, 'There'll be a run for you on the off-side if you want it.' Some of the Leicester team told me years later that they had argued with Les against giving me the run. They said that one day I might make a lot of runs against them, and they should not encourage me. But on that day, I scored the run they gave me, and one more unaided, before being dismissed the second time. And I still had not received a ball from Jack Walsh, nor recognised which one was Watson.

* * *

As a youngster, 'Bomber' Wells played his first match for Gloucestershire at Bristol against Sussex. Their great off-spin bowler, Tom Goddard, had just retired and 'Bomber' was taking his place. I rather think I was his first wicket. He bowled some 40 overs, His run-up to bowl took three paces. Back in the Gloucester dressing room, this new recruit said, 'Well, I can see that I am going to have to do a lot of bowling. I think I must cut down my run.'

In 1960, when I was playing an occasional match for Sussex, a number of cricketers had started calling me 'Rev'. I was batting against Nottinghamshire at Trent Bridge, for whom 'Bomber' Wells was now playing. I edged a ball from him rather luckily past slip. He called down the pitch, 'Said your prayers well last night, Rev!'

I called back, 'Why didn't you say your prayers last night, Bomber?'

'No,' he said. 'I trust to luck.'

NED SHERRIN

—◇—

Film, theatre and television producer, presenter, director and writer, Ned Sherrin CBE has a list of credits which includes That Was The Week That Was, Side By Side By Sondheim *and* Loose Ends.

These lyrics are by John Arlott, commissioned by the BBC for the Radio Three programme *The Sound Of Cricket* in 1979. It was performed by the Yetties, who also wrote the music. Harold Gimblett was Somerset's greatest ever – and they didn't even include him on the Centenary Commemorative Plate!

HAROLD GIMBLETT'S HUNDRED

Bicknoller was his village, Harold Gimblett was his name,
Farming was his working day, but cricket was his game.
When he was but twenty, and first played for Somerset,
He played the mighty innings, that we remember yet.

CHORUS: Oh! He struck them with skill, and he struck
   them with power,
Times out of number he gave them Stogumber
And knocked up a century in just on the hour.

Stogumber is the village where Jack White used to live,
But for cricketers in Somerset, that's the name they give
To the fierce cross-batted stroke they will use forever more,
Swinging it right off the stumps, and past long leg for four.

Young Gimblett went to Taunton to have a county trial.
John Daniell broke the news to him, they did not like his
   style.
Then a man cried off, and he was called back to the room.
'You'll play for us tomorrow, against Essex, down at Frome.'

On May 18th, '35, at six he left the farm
On the way to catch the bus, his cricket bag under his arm.
Soon to drink pavilion tea, though he felt a little grim,
With cricketers who up till then, had been but names to him.

Somerset had Ingle, the two Lees, Frank and Jack
The famous Farmer White and Arthur Wellard in attack.
For Essex – Pearce, O'Connor, the Smiths, Peter and Ray,
Eastman, Wade and Cutmore – they all were there
   that day.

There was Nichols of England too – the mighty 'Maurice
    Nick'.
His arms were long, his shoulders wide, his pace was
    mighty quick.
When Somerset went into bat, his slips held all the snicks.
The score, when Gimblett's turn came round, was 107 for 6.

The crowd had never heard of him, they did not know
    his name
But since he was from Somerset, they clapped him just
    the same.
They saw him miss the spin of Smith, but very quickly
    then,
For a single, pushed off Nichols, they clapped him once
    again.

In with Arthur Wellard, biggest hitter of them all,
Young Gimblett soon outscored him – he was middling
    the ball.
When Smith tossed up his googly, that ball of mystery,
He landed it Stogumber, on top of the old marquee!

Wellard went and Luckes came – Gimblett reached his fifty.
Luckes was out, Andrews then, played it cool and thrifty.
Nichols took the bright new ball, and Gimblett drove
    him straight;
When he dropped it short, he hooked him, and cut him
    neat and late.

The chilly crowd had watched him while he had changed
    the game,
And now they felt they knew him, and they shouted out
    his name.
For one fine savage over, Nichols checked his score,

But then the young man cracked him through the old
   pavilion door.

A different situation fell on the Frome ground then,
Because the tins there only marked the score up ten
   by ten.
Of tension in the dressing room, the team could give
   no sign,
There was no way of telling him his score was ninety-nine!

But Nichols bowled and Gimblett then drove him clean
   for four.
He'd done it – scored a century – the crowd let out a
   roar.
And to this day you may read it, it's in the record books,
An hour and just three minutes is all the time he took.

That night, all through Somerset, from Minehead 'cross
   to Street,
Bristol down to Wellington, they talked of this great feat,
And thousands ever since have claimed that they were
   there to see
Harold Gimblett, from Bicknoller, make cricket history.

DENNIS SILK

*Former Somerset cricketer, President of MCC and
Chairman of TCCB in the 1990s, Dennis Silk CBE was
Warden of Radley College for many years.*

Charlie Harris, the delightfully capricious Notts opening
bat before and just after the Second World War, was in the

habit, when fielding in the gully, of taking out his false teeth and placing them in the 'open' position on the ground beside him. He would then remark, in a hoarse whisper to the batsman as the bowler ran up, 'Be careful my son. There are two of us waiting to gobble you up.'

The same Charlie Harris once dived to take a catch in the gully and dislocated his shoulder. He was carted off to Trent Bridge Hospital, where a large matron laid him out on the floor and tried to put his shoulder back. In his agony, he shouted and screamed.

Matron stood back and said, 'Mr Harris, you are a coward. There is a young girl next door who has just had twins and she hasn't uttered a sound.'

Charlie Harris thought about this for a moment and said, 'Aye love, but just you wait till you start trying to put them back in again.'

ALAN SIMPSON

<o>

With Ray Galton, Alan Simpson OBE is one of the greatest television comedy writers. Together they created Hancock's Half Hour *for Tony Hancock, and* Steptoe and Son, *two of the best loved and most successful British TV comedy programmes of all time.*

This is a true story. I was there. Stamford Bridge, Saturday 27th August 1955. Three months earlier Chelsea had won the League Championship for the first and so far only time in their history. Today is the first match of the new season for the newly crowned champions. Versus Bolton Wanderers.

Suddenly, unannounced, at 2.30 the Chelsea team in full kit runs onto the field carrying the Championship Shield and do a lap of honour to a tumultuous reception from the 65,000 crowd. Round the running track they trot, pandemonium at every stride, grown men are crying. Back to the dressing room they go.

At 2.50 out they come again to another tumultuous reception, this time for the team photo with the Shield. Back in they go.

Five minutes later out they come for the third time to yet another tumultuous reception. The captains toss up. Nat Lofthouse wins the toss. Chelsea kick-off.

Roy Bentley taps the ball to his inside left, and a bloke two yards away from me bawls out, 'Same old bleedin' Chelsea!'

REG SIMPSON

<><o><>

Nottinghamshire and England opening batsman,
who played 27 times for England between 1948 and
1954. He scored over 30,000 runs and hit
64 centuries in his career.

During the MCC tour to Australia in 1950/51, on one particular occasion we were flying between two destinations in a Dakota. The crew became acquainted with the fact that I had flown Dakotas as a pilot for nearly 1,200 hours. As a result, they invited me to sit in the First Pilot's seat and asked me to keep an eye on things while they went back to talk to Denis Compton and others.

Eric Hollies, the Warwickshire leg-spinner who bowled Bradman for a duck in his final Test innings, hated flying.

When he saw the flight crew in the passenger compartment, he asked them who was flying the aircraft. Someone apparently said, 'Reg', so Eric rushed to the front. The next thing I knew the cabin door was flung open and Eric stood in the entrance with a horrified look on his face.

'What are you doing?' he shouted.

'Just keeping an eye on everything,' I replied.

Obviously, he did not appreciate the fact that 'George' the automatic pilot, as we called it, was operating, and he returned to his seat for a stiff whisky. For the remainder of the tour, he did his best to avoid flying. I can't recall whether or not he succeeded.

DONALD SINDEN

Distinguished actor whose career has spanned almost the entire post-war period. Sir Donald's most distinguished work has been done on the stage, but his film appearances include The Cruel Sea *and* Doctor In The House *and his television credits include* Two's Company *and* Never The Twain.

Noel Coward bequeathed me his very splendid shooting stick with his initials – N.C. – emblazoned on the leather. This was very useful when I was suffering from arthritis, as it meant I could perch wherever I was. I took it to Lord's and in the tea interval, an elderly member of MCC asked me why I needed a stick. Having explained, I proudly asked, 'Whose initials do you think they are?'

Tears welled up in his eyes. 'Not Neville Cardus!'

I failed to think of a good riposte.

KEITH SMITH

Popular after-dinner speaker at sports events.

I was at a sports charity function, and was speaking to a Chelsea FC director, who told me that the club had recently been burgled.

'Did the burglars take any cups?' I asked.

'No,' he replied. 'They never went near the kitchen.'

I told that story at the annual Stag Dinner of the Vaudeville Golfing Society, when I was captain in 1994. David Mellor was a guest speaker and Ken Bates the guest of honour. David Mellor loved it, but Ken Bates was a bit tight-lipped!

MIKE SMITH

M.J.K. Smith was one of England's last double internationals, having played both cricket and rugby for England. His cricket career was more distinguished: he captained England in 25 of his 50 Tests.

I was the manager of the England tour to West Indies in 1993/94. We came to the Fifth Test at Antigua, where Brian Lara made 375. Robin Smith made a big hundred for us and we were hanging in there.

The time came for Phil 'The Cat' Tufnell to go to the wicket. Not known for troubling the scorers too long, or for showing any enthusiasm in facing anything above medium pace, he knew the quickies would be queueing up to bowl. He was immediately lbw to Winston Benjamin – not the quickest of the West Indies' bowlers – for a duck.

The ball looked leg-side to me, and I commiserated with Cat to this effect.

'I'm very pleased to hear you say that,' he replied. 'I never reckon to get in line.'

FRANCIS STAFFORD

Francis, Lord Stafford inherited his ancient title on the death of his father in 1986. In 1997 he established The Lord Stafford Awards to encourage collaborative relationships between Staffordshire business and universities. He is President of the North West region of the Lord's Taverners.

I played one of my first Lord's Taverners cricket matches at the picturesque ground at Stratford upon Avon when I was Francis Fitzherbert, before I became Lord Stafford.

On the list of players that day we had all the illustrious names of television and sport including Terry Wogan, Sir David Frost, Colin (later Lord) Cowdrey, Rory Bremner, M.J.K. Smith, Chris Tarrant and so on – and then me.

It was only when I changed into my cricket whites that I heard people whispering, '... and who is he?'

Just as we took the field, two ladies marched up and asked who I was and what I did. Unable to compete with my fellow celebrities, I said I did nothing really.

They then put N.E. by my name and walked off. I ran after them and enquired what N.E. stood for.

'Oh,' they said. 'That stands for Non Entity!'

Whenever I can, I now sign myself The Lord Stafford N.E.

JOHN STAPLETON

—◄○►—

Very experienced television journalist and presenter, well known for BBC TV's Watchdog, *with his wife Lynne Faulds Wood. Also a news presenter on GMTV.*

I have blue blood – sky-blue blood. Like my grandfather, my father and the son I've brainwashed, I am a Manchester City fan. We've not had much to shout about for the last 20-odd years. But once a Blue, always a Blue. So when City were at Spurs in 2003/04 and I was unable to get to the game, I sat down to watch it on Sky TV.

By half-time, we were 3–nil down. Having been up since 4 a.m. (I present GMTV every morning) and having taken the usual anaesthetic (from a bottle of chardonnay), I stormed

193

off to bed denouncing my side's performance as humiliating – or words to that effect.

And as followers of the game will know, I missed the greatest comeback of the season, if not the decade, as my team miraculously scored four goals, the last coming in Roy of the Rovers style in the final minute.

SHEILA STEAFEL

━━━━━━━━━━◀◯▶━━━━━━━━━━

South African-born comedy actress who has appeared with all the great comedy names of the past 30 years – Frankie Howerd, John Cleese, Ronnie Barker and Beryl Reid among many others.

I was in love. Hopelessly, blindly, in love. Tall and distinctly plain, Douglas oozed charm, as consummate conmen do. I knew it and I didn't care. I was totally Svengali-ed. I would follow him doggedly around the golf course at a respectful distance, stooping under the weight of his heavy bag of clubs and doting on his sturdy legs and broad be-cardiganed back as he squared up to the ball.

'Dear girl,' he said to me one day as I heaved his golf bag into the boot of my small car, 'you really should learn to play. They'd love you, in your little tartan skirt and white ankle socks, hair neatly tied back. Goodness, never mind them, I'd find it pretty sexy!'

Say no more. For the next three months I fought a losing battle with that mean little white ball and the iron sticks I'd been given by a retired aunt.

'But they're right-handed,' I whined, 'and I'm left-handed.'

'Dear girl, what an advantage!' Douglas beamed and patted my rear. 'You'll have an enormously strong follow-through.'

I persisted. My golfing instructor persisted. Useless. Determinedly I tried, but the divots flew and I cried with frustration.

'How are you getting along, old thing?'

'Improving,' I lied.

I was, as usual, chauffeuring him, this time to pick up his newly serviced car.

'Tell you what! I take it you've got your clubs with you?'

I had been ordered to keep them handy at all times, in case.

'Of course,' I answered miserably.

'Well, there's a nine-holer on the way. We'll stop off, have a round and see how you are doing.'

Short of crashing the car, there was nothing to be done. I pulled into the car park.

'I'll hire a set for myself,' Douglas said over his shoulder, setting off briskly towards the golf shop alongside the course. I hauled the ugly canvas bag out of the car boot and followed him.

'Come on, old thing,' he called, and then turned round to look at me. 'Dear girl,' he said, 'you're shivering.'

I was. I hadn't anticipated a round of golf that morning, and the chiffon blouse and elegant skirt I was wearing ('Don't wear jeans, old thing. Always try to look elegant.') weren't exactly suitable for the chilly autumn weather.

'No no, I'm fine!' I smiled grimly, trying to control my shivers.

'Come along,' he said briskly, and entering the shop strode up to the counter where a young salesman stood. The wall behind him was decorated with sweaters, patterned and plain, bright and subdued, all pinned up in alarming positions.

'Hmmm.' Douglas scratched his chin thoughtfully. Then he turned to me. 'What do you think of that one on the left?' He pointed.

'Oh my goodness, I thought. He's actually going to buy me a present. At last! This man whom I adored in spite of his tight-fistedness was finally going to show some affection, some consideration, and buy me a sweater! I felt ashamed: I had misjudged him all this time. Opening a drawer, the assistant took out an identical sweater and handed it to Douglas.

'Ye-e-es.' He held it up for me to inspect. 'What do you think?'

'Lovely!' I breathed.

'Splendid.'

Then he handed it to me, pulled off his own sweater, and taking the new one out of my incredulous hands, gave me the one he'd just removed.

'You can borrow that,' he said with a generous smile, 'until we get back to my flat.'

Next day the clubs went to Oxfam.

DAVID STEELE

—◄○►—

*Northamptonshire and England batsman who
transformed English cricket's morale as 'the bank clerk
who went to war' in 1975, against the Australians. He
won almost everything that year – BBC's Sports
Personality Of The Year, and 365 meat chops from a
grateful butcher, one for every Test run he scored.*

Fred Jakeman, a Yorkshireman, played for Northamptonshire in the early 1950s. He was a left-handed batsman and did not like batting against Doug Wright, the great Kent and England leg-spinner. He used to have nightmares thinking about him.

Playing against Kent at Dover, Fred was sitting in the pavilion waiting to bat, nervously smoking a cigarette, when a wicket fell and one of his team-mates said, 'You're in, Fred.'

He strode out of the pavilion still smoking his cigarette, but in his nervousness he had forgotten to take his bat with him. He came back into the pavilion, put down his cigarette and picked up his bat, and marched back out to the middle. He was then, not surprisingly, out first ball, so he was able to come back to the pavilion and finish smoking his cigarette.

In cricket, most of the trouble is in the mind.

ANDY STEGGALL

━━━━━━━◄○►━━━━━━━

*Sports journalist and broadcaster
for ITV's* Meridian Tonight.

In November 1983, as a young sports reporter I got my break. My first big assignment in local radio was covering British middleweight boxer Tony Sibson's world title fight against the defending champion 'Marvelous' (one L is correct) Marvin Hagler. It was such a big event for his home town Leicester that a plane was chartered to take fight fans to Worcester, Massachusetts, in the USA to see the epic, and I went with them.

The local radio station, Centre Radio, went about the build-up with gusto. The morning DJ and I interviewed the passengers and played their favourite music before they boarded. But the grand finale was the moment East Midlands Airport opened up the control tower to the DJ and the cockpit to me. The moment we took off we began talking. Unfortunately the static at my end meant I couldn't hear certain words, which as it turned out proved pretty crucial. The DJ asked me, 'Andy, we saw you with the fight fans, a few broken noses, a few cauliflower ears among those on board.'

Then came the bit I didn't hear: 'But are there any women with you?'

And my reply was, 'Yes, there are some real old pros.'

Sibbo lost, and I only just survived!

RICHARD STILGOE

—◄○►—

Musical entertainer, lyricist of the musical
Starlight Express *and others, and President of*
the Lord's Taverners from 2003 to 2004.

We were playing for the Lord's Taverners against the local team on the tiny Channel Island of Sark, and I was bowling. Rather to my surprise, a wicket fell and the new man strode to the crease, looking very mature and imposing.

I turned to the umpire and asked him who the new batsman was.

'He's the Seneschal of Sark,' came the reply.

'What's a Seneschal?' I asked.

'He's the only judge and magistrate on the island, and President of Chief Pleas,' came the reply.

'Ah,' I said. 'But what about his cricketing skills? Is there anything else I should know about him?'

'Yes,' said the umpire. 'He's my cousin. So there's no point in you appealing.'

T

CHRIS TARRANT

—◄○►—

Radio and television broadcaster who made his name on Tiswas *and became a household name through his hosting of* Who Wants To Be A Millionaire?

There's a strange look that taxi drivers give you when they recognise you, but don't want to embarrass you by saying anything. It's a series of strange looks and half winks in their mirror at you in the back. If you're trying to read a paper or whatever, it's strangely unnerving and you never quite settle without feeling watched.

I was going from Capital Radio to the Oval for an interview on *Test Match Special* in a cab last year, and the driver kept half winking and nodding at me all the way out of town towards Kennington, without actually saying a word.

When I finally got out at LWT, I tried to give him a fiver (the fare was actually only £4.90 but I thought 'what the hell'!), but he wouldn't hear of it.

'No, no, no,' he said. 'I want you to keep that. I wouldn't dream of taking it off you. I just want to say a sincere thank you on behalf of me, my wife and my family and kids for all the sheer pleasure you've brought us over the years – on TV, radio, records, books, commercials ...

And above all, for the wonderful work that you do at Stoke Mandeville Hospital.'

CHRIS TAVARE

——◄○►——

Kent, Somerset and England batsman, known for his reliability and the lack of urgency to his batting. Played 31 times for England in the 1980s, and finished with a career record of almost 25,000 runs and 48 hundreds.

Kent played Hampshire at Canterbury in a Championship match at the beginning of 1978, when Andy Roberts was one of their overseas players. He was one of the West Indies' most fearsome fast bowlers. He was known to bowl a slow bouncer to give batsmen a false sense of security, followed by a quick bouncer, one of which had knocked out Colin Cowdrey at Basingstoke a few years earlier. I remembered playing for the Combined Universities against the West Indies two years earlier, walking out to bat and passing Peter Roebuck returning to the pavilion with a big 'egg' protruding from the middle of his forehead, the result of another Roberts exocet. We were not looking forward to the experience of facing Mr Roberts.

Hampshire batted first, and when Roberts came in, he had the most almighty slog, causing a twinge in his right shoulder. The Kent physio, an ex Marine, told him, 'I wouldn't bowl with that', and Roberts took his advice, much to our relief. He only bowled seven overs in the entire match, which Kent won by four wickets.

The physio told us later that there was, in fact, very little wrong with his shoulder!

SHAW TAYLOR

————◄○►————

Announcer, quizmaster, chat-show host, sports commentator, DJ and presenter of Police Five, *ITV's crime show which ran for 30 years from the 1960s to the 1990s.*

Close on fifty years ago, when ITV started, sports commentators were in short supply, outside of the BBC. The ITV commentary problem was, in the main, solved by teaming up your 'telly pro' with a 'sporting expert', and the double act worked well, in most cases. We followed the television commentators' Golden Rule: don't tell the viewer what he can see for himself. If you can't add to the picture, shut up.

When I covered the Ice-Skating Championships, I was teamed up with ex-champion Malcolm Cannon, and we complemented each other perfectly: I could add to the picture the skater's background, personality and past history, while Malcolm supplied the expert opinion on the quality of the skating. We reckoned viewers fell into two groups – those who knew their skating and didn't need every step identified, and ordinary viewers who couldn't tell a Double Salchow from a Triple Toe Loop but simply enjoyed the spectacle and the music. A running commentary would be wasted on one, and drive the other barmy. Imagine being at the ballet with the guy behind whispering in your ear, 'Beautiful entrechat … and two glissades in a row!' You'd tell him to glissade off.

We applied the system to all sorts of sports and other

interests – ten-pin bowling, contract bridge, ballroom dancing, water-ski championships, and even hovercraft racing.

The one time it came unstuck was when I received a phone call from Thames TV's Head of Outside Broadcasts, Graham Turner.

'You play snooker, don't you, Shaw?'

'Well, yes,' I said, wondering what was coming.

'Good. We're covering a snooker series and we haven't got a commentator. And don't worry,' said Graham airily. 'You'll have an expert with you.'

I don't recall the name of the 'expert with me' but he wasn't an ex-champion and hardly knew more than me. I quickly discovered that second guessing what a snooker player is going for, and why, just ain't that easy.

I gathered, from what was said to me afterwards by the man in the street, that the only thing my commentary added to the picture was raucous hilarity in snooker clubs up and down the country – and in some, no doubt, stuttering rage. It seems that my snooker programme became compulsive viewing.

'It were great, lad,' said one fan. 'I haven't laughed so much in years. You know bugger all about it, don't you?'

STAN TAYLOR

—◄○►—

The 'Submarine' man, for many years Stan Taylor has been recognised as one of the top after-dinner speakers in Great Britain, and a master of dialect humour.

An elderly golfer was talking to his chums in the locker room. 'I get backache after eighteen holes nowadays, but the osteopath always puts me right in no time!'

One of his playing partners said, 'I remember your grand-dad used to have a bad back too.'

'Yes,' said the old golfer, 'in the 1930s they used to inject mercury into your spine to cure backache. They did this to my granddad in 1932, when he was over 60.'

'Did it work?'

'Oh yes. In the hot weather he was eight foot six tall. And in the cold weather they carried him round in a bucket.'

ROBERT TEAR

Noted tenor and conductor, Robert Tear CBE
has credits which include Billy Budd *with the Welsh*
National Orchestra, many performances at the Royal
Opera House, Covent Garden, and many recordings.

It's a beautiful day at a small cricket ground in Bath. We are playing a charity match. I am fielding in the outfield and there is a flash of Ian Botham's bat. The ball is coming my way, never more than six feet off the ground, whirring like a partridge.

I drop it.

Sarah Potter, the bowler, knows how to cheer a man up. 'If you had caught that, it would have been the best day of my life.'

I cannot look her in the eye. Shame rules. A cloud covers the sun.

GARY TEICHMANN

South African number 8 who played 42 times for the
Springboks between 1995 and 1999, captaining the
team in 36 of his games. He led South Africa to a then
record 17 consecutive international victories.

There comes a time in every player's career when one has to make that decision about when the right time is to retire. It is not an easy decision, especially if you have been playing for a long period. There are always signs on the field that will give you some idea. We were playing in Dunedin when our centre, Dick Muir, got a break and was heading straight for the try line with no full back in place. Out the corner of his eye he saw his centre partner calling for him to make the pass. He could not understand why and had a glance out his right-hand side and saw this figure catching up to him very quickly. He was about to make the pass when this figure overtook him. It was a young up-and-coming touch judge who was underneath the poles way before him. It was not long after that he decided to retire.

* * *

John Allan, the Scottish/SA hooker, is known for his passion – especially when running onto the field. He always runs on with great pace, overtaking the captain long before you are on the field. At Eden Park in New Zealand, the changing rooms are positioned behind the north side of the field. Before our first ever game there, John did not go out onto the field. I ended up winning the toss and decided we would play towards the changing rooms.

As usual, as we ran out John came sprinting past me and the rest of the team before we had even come out from under the stands and reached the field. It was probably at this point that he realised that he had a whole half of the field still to cover, and he had to carry on at top speed – he couldn't lose face in front of the vast All Black crowd.

By the time we got to him, he was out of breath before the ball had even been kicked.

LESLIE THOMAS

Author and QPR fanatic. Since the success of
The Virgin Soldiers, *he has been a best-selling author,
and his detective books, featuring Dangerous Davies,
have been turned into a television series.*

When I was in my early twenties, I used to play soccer two or
three times a week. I was a reporter on the local newspaper in
Willesden, north-west London, and I not only played in the
matches but also wrote the reports. So I never had a bad game.
Once we lost 13–1, and after summarising briefly the other
side's 13 goals, I devoted four paragraphs to my brilliant solo
effort.

Mike Selvey, of Middlesex and England, tells how he once went to Lord's early in January to wish some of the office girls a Happy New Year. The gatekeeper, however, refused to let him in on account of neither Middlesex nor England having a match that day.

BILL THRELFALL

Leading tennis commentator for 30 years, Bill also played at Wimbledon in the 1950s, and has won the National Veterans' Championships five times.

The scene – the Hard Court Tennis Championships of Great Britain, 1955. I was playing in the event, but at the time was watching a very exciting men's doubles with my wife in the stands on Centre Court. The match included a couple of players who knew us (and our small Yorkshire terrier) well. During an exciting rally, our little dog, having escaped from our car in the car park, hurtled on to the court. Cleverly reacting to the sound of balls being hit, he ran around the court checking on each player to no avail. A player who knew us, and where we were sitting, picked him up and brought him into the stand.

The dog got more applause than anybody that day.

BILL TIDY

<o>

A great cartoonist, wit and sports nut.

I once dug a large hole at the NEC Metropole Hotel. The dinner was the first major function organised by two young lasses, and as the speaker, I arrived early to find them both very anxious about the outcome. To them it was a really important milestone, to me it was just another dinner so, oozing paternal confidence, I embraced them and said, 'You have no worries! The tables are set, your guests will come back from hacking round The Belfry in brilliant sunshine to boast that they've played a world-class golf course, and your speaker is here! Relax, nip upstairs and put your party frocks on!'

'We've got them on!'

*   *   *

In my early Taverner days, one of my original drawings would sometimes be placed among the 'Choose Your Own' section of the raffle prizes. This practice terminated the night I watched a winner look at my deathless artwork and then at an adjacent Bee Gees LP. The turmoil in his mind was frightening to behold, and a haemorrhage seemed only seconds away. Then he saw the beautifully wrapped bunch of asparagus …

ALAN TITCHMARSH

<o>

*Hugely popular television gardening expert
and novelist, a man who sends ladies of a certain
age into paroxysms of delight.*

The only time I ever caused a stir on the cricket field was
when I was at Ilkley County Secondary School and I ran out
to take the opening batsman his box. He'd left it in the
dressing room, so he beckoned me over and whispered in
my ear.

211

'Fetch us me box, Fred – it's somewhere in the dressing room.' (They used my middle name as my nickname at school. With a surname like Titchmarsh it could have been worse, but fortunately my older cousin was already known as Titty. I was called Fred to avoid confusion.)

I went to the dressing room, eventually located the protective item under a pile of evil-smelling socks, and ran out onto the field, waving it over my head to signify my success. The straps streamed out behind me like a banner, and the batsman snatched it from me with a red face and stuffed it down his trousers. You'd have thought he'd have been grateful.

Half a dozen girls on the boundary line lay on their backs, kicking their legs in the air, and laughed until they cried.

SAM TORRANCE

<o>

Scottish golfer, captain of Britain and Europe's victorious Ryder Cup team in 2002, of which he has been a crucial part since 1981.

Fellow pro Simon Hobday tells a story about when he was travelling late to an event in the States and was stopped on the freeway going at 110 mph. Simon pulled over and saw a huge macho American cop strolling towards his car.

The cop bent down towards Simon and drawled, 'Goddam my boy – I have been waiting all day for someone like you', to which Simon replied, 'Well, I got here as quick as I could'!!

TIM TREMLETT

—◇—

*Former Hampshire cricketer who has gone on to become
a leading cricket coach. Both his father Maurice and his
son Chris have also played county cricket.*

In June 1985 Hampshire were riding high in the
Championship thanks to the talents of the likes of Gordon
Greenidge and Malcolm Marshall.

Following morning practice in Southampton, I travelled
to Birmingham with my room-mate, Bobby Parks, on the
way to play our Championship match versus Warwickshire
at Edgbaston. The weather was good but both of us had
summer colds and we were not helped by the fact that we
were driving the team's kit van, whose maximum speed was
40 miles per hour!

On this particular occasion we were staying at a hotel in West Bromwich, a good half an hour's drive from Edgbaston. We went to bed at a respectable hour, as normal, put in an early morning call for 7.30 a.m. and went to sleep.

On the Saturday morning we woke and, as always, as a good room-mate, Bobby was up first to make my early morning cup of tea and draw the curtains. It was a lovely, bright, sunny morning with not a cloud in the sky, but as we had not been woken up by our hotel's morning call, we wondered what time it was. Bobby duly turned on the television to check the little clock in the corner of the television. A look of horror appeared on his face, one that I usually associated with when it was his turn at the bar and his team-mates all turned up at the same time! However, on this occasion, he hurriedly dived across the bed to check his watch and, sure enough, it confirmed that it was 10.10 a.m. Oops!! Here we were a good half an hour away with all the team's kit standing in the hotel's car park.

We grabbed our clothes, hurriedly got dressed in the corridor and lift, and rushed through reception asking them to phone the ground to explain that we would be rather late but would get there as soon as possible. Bob had already started the kit van up and was halfway across the car park when I caught up with him having relayed the message.

Driving through Hansworth, we were stopped at a roundabout with Bob just about to pull out when suddenly we were hit from the rear. Both of us ended up knocking our heads on the windscreen. Dazed (although I think the knock has helped Bob over the years), we got out of the car to take the driver's details and check that all his passengers were OK. I say 'all' because there was an Indian family of about seven in the car, including lots of little children. Fortunately, no one was seriously hurt. We exchanged pleasantries and addresses and continued on our journey.

Eventually we reached Edgbaston and were greeted by about half the side, news having been passed to the dressing room via the main gate. No mobile phones in those days!

Our captain, Mark Nicholas, showing remarkable composure, quickly explained that the match would start five minutes late. The likes of Chris Smith and Gordon Greenidge were busy knocking some balls into the advertising boards in their civvies when we reached the dressing room. Mark, in the meantime, went out to toss the coin, which sadly went against us, and to the disgruntlement of the rest of the team we trudged onto the field under the blue skies and in the already considerable morning heat.

The pitch was flat and Warwickshire progressed rather steadily. However, after about 25 minutes one of the openers pushed forward to Malcolm Marshall, duly got an edge, and the ball went at a comfortable height to wicket-keeper Bobby. Much to the consternation of the close fielders, Bobby did a bad impression of a percussionist playing the cymbals, and the ball dropped to the ground.

However, we did manage to take a couple of wickets, and in strode the mighty Dennis Amiss who, as normal, appeared unhurried and in good form. There was only one fielder at this stage on the off-side, namely me, who had crept into the cover position. A quarter of an hour later and Dennis drove at one a little bit early and sliced it to my position at cover, where I nonchalantly lined up the ball for a catch but disastrously got it wrong: the ball went through my fingers, hit me on the chest and ricocheted for two runs. My team-mates were not sure whether to laugh or cry, although looking at Malcolm's face I could sense what he was thinking, and an invitation to join him for dinner was not on the list.

Just when you thought things couldn't get any worse, a couple of overs later I chased the ball to the mid-off boundary. In those days, Edgbaston was not as developed as it is now and there were some railings underneath the big scoreboard. I chased the ball as fast as I could, which is not saying much as my father always compared my running style to a one-legged duck. However, I managed to stop the ball just inside the boundary, flicked it back in true Jonty Rhodes fashion, and jumped the advertising board before nearly impaling myself on the railings. Twisting round like Zinedine Zidane I set off to retrieve the ball. Unfortunately, my spikes slipped on the concrete supporting the railings, and as my right leg screwed backwards my ankle got stuck between two of the railings with the Warwickshire batsmen continuing to run between the wickets. I managed to get free but by the time I had done, the umpires had to confer to count how many runs the Warwickshire batsmen had actually scored.

Fortunately, this was the last of the calamities, as we somehow managed to bowl Warwickshire out for 130.

Gordon Greenidge went on to make a double century and if it had not been for the weather – it rained continuously from lunchtime on the third day – we would have pulled off a remarkable innings victory.

At the end of the match, Parks and Tremlett received a bollocking from M.C.J. Nicholas. We continued to drive the kit van, but were never late again!

FRED TRUEMAN

—◄○►—

*Indisputably England's greatest fast bowler
since the Second World War, Fiery Fred took 307 Test
wickets, which was then a world record. He then became
a well-known commentator on BBC radio's*
Test Match Special *for many years.*

It is said in Yorkshire that the eminent writer, E.W. Swanton of *The Daily Telegraph*, on an occasion when his car broke down, was looking around for assistance. In due course he flagged down an oncoming car, which happened to be a Rolls Royce.

The driver was a local farmer and told Jim he would take him to a nearby village garage. On the journey Jim got into conversation with the farmer, and asked why he had a glass partition between the front and rear seats.

The farmer replied, 'It is very useful. It stops the sheep from licking my neck on the way back from the market.'

CHRISTINE TRUMAN JANES

━━━━━━━━━━━◄O►━━━━━━━━━━━

The only British woman to have been seeded number one at Wimbledon since the Second World War, Christine Truman lost in the 1961 Final to Angela Mortimer in three sets after injuring her leg falling on the court during the match. She is now a respected commentator on her sport.

When Max Robertson and I were commentating on a Wimbledon Men's Doubles match on Centre Court a few years back, Max asked me who the winners were due to play in the final.

I said, 'Max, this is the Final!'

STUART TURNER

*After-Dinner Speaker of the Year award winner,
British Rally Champion navigator for two years, won the
RAC Rally with Eric Carlsson, and author of 20 books
on motor sport and business, including his
autobiography 'Twice Lucky'.*

When we were having an ushers' briefing at Graham Hill's funeral, someone said that a member of the public was praying where family members were due to be seated.

Henry Cooper smacked one huge fist into another and said, 'Shall I go and have a word with him?'

Graham would have liked that.

218

JULIAN TUTT

———◄○►———

*BBC golf commentator, journalist and broadcaster, he is
the whispering voice of the fairways and bunkers for
Radio Five Live and BBC television.*

While preparing for the following day's Royal British Legion
Festival of Remembrance in the Royal Albert Hall, I had
locked myself away in an upstairs room, warning security
that I would be late leaving. Having finally finished my
notes, I came out at midnight to find the Hall bathed in
light, but not a sign of human life. Having done two circuits
of the Hall and found every exit (including the Artiste's)
firmly locked and bolted, and not a security man in sight,
I started to panic. With a long and demanding day to follow,
I faced a night kipping beside the Great Organ.

But first, this was too good an opportunity to miss. I took
to the stage where so many great names have performed,
and with bursting lungs gave vent to 'The hills are alive with
the sound of muuu-sic!', plus the odd trumpet solo with a
borrowed instrument left carelessly lying around.

Eventually, having exhausted my repertoire, I found the
PA system and announced my plight to anyone who might
be there. After five minutes a sleepy-eyed security man
appeared, looking even more surprised than me. He'd been
fast asleep and hadn't heard a thing!

I finally got to bed at 1.30 a.m., shaken and a little stirred.

V

PETER VAUGHAN

—◄◦►—

*Actor known for his range of sympathetic villains,
from Grouty in* Porridge *to Magwitch in* Great
Expectations. *He also played Anthony Hopkins'
father in* The Remains Of The Day, *not to
mention roles in* Straw Dogs *and* The French
Lieutenant's Woman *among many others.*

In the 60s I was lucky enough to play for Vic Lewis' charity
Sunday side. The team was a mixture of cricketers and lesser
mortals like me from the world of entertainment. One week,
John Reid, the New Zealand captain and one of the great
gully fielders of all time, turned out for us.

We fielded first, and to my chagrin Vic said to John, 'Pete
always fields in the gully. Would you go in the slips?'

The first ball flashed past me at catchable height. I reacted
at about the same time as the umpire signalled four.

Reid turned to me and enquired, 'What's up mate? Didn't
you realise the game had started?'

I swapped places there and then, but at least I can say I was preferred in the gully to John Reid, even if only for one ball!

DEBRA VEAL

—◄○►—

*The oarswoman who carried on rowing
across the Atlantic alone when her husband, a 6ft 5"
international oarsman, left the boat early in the voyage.
Debra Veal MBE saw no reason to stop and rowed on to
become only the third woman in the world to
have rowed an ocean solo.*

THE WOES OF AN OCEAN ROWER

It took three months to row across the Atlantic, during which time I never did get over the sight of a flying fish! Flying at high speeds they seemed to come from nowhere. When the big ones hit they hurt as much as being given a dead-arm punch, just like those delivered in playgrounds worldwide. Although most of the flying fish were tiny and just bounced off, they could still be a nuisance, especially when I was eating or if they dropped into my lap while I was rowing naked.

Dorados, on the other hand, are one cool species of fish. They would swim along with me for miles and miles, and they eat flying fish – a bonus as far as I was concerned! Most of them were about a metre in length and the most beautiful bright blue, with glowing green-yellow fins and tails. They cleared the water at a great height as they leapt out and slammed back down in an attempt to remove parasites. Considering the size and weight of these beasties (my oh-so-handy little fish book told me they can weigh up to 40 kilos) some of them cleared two to three metres above the water level and would land with an almighty splash.

One night they were going for it big time, as if they were taking part in the Dorado High Jump Championships, so I decided to try to photograph them. They stay airborne for quite some time so I figured that if I could just get the camera pointing in vaguely the right direction I could get a good photo. Nice idea in theory, but I now have a new-found respect for wildlife photographers.

Every time I set myself up looking out over the port side I would hear a splash and turn just in time to catch a whopper landing from an epic leap on the starboard side. After this had happened a few times I switched to the starboard side, only for all of the leaping action to switch to the port side.

I'm convinced it was a Dorado conspiracy – 'Operation Photo Avoidance'. One of the lesser leapers was on watch, reporting back to the rest of the team. I could almost imagine the radio call:

'Bravo this is Alpha, target is mobile ... now static on the port side. All stations, switch to starboard side – GO, GO, GO!'

BRIAN VINER

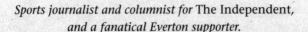

Sports journalist and columnist for The Independent, *and a fanatical Everton supporter.*

A colleague of mine on *The Independent* was in Marseilles during the 1998 World Cup and found himself in a square just as some England fans went on the rampage. He phoned the newsdesk and they asked him for 500 words, but told him to make it snappy as the first editions were ready to roll. Ten minutes later he filed his report to a copytaker, who seemed only half-engaged in the job, doubtless because she thought she was about to knock off for the day. As it was so close to deadline there was no time for a sub-editor to read the piece through.

In the line delivered to the copytaker, my colleague said that 'the troublemakers scattered when a van pulled up containing 10 armed gendarmes'. The line printed in the paper the following morning was, 'the troublemakers scattered when a van pulled up containing 10 armed John Barnes'.

But I wouldn't want people to think that it is only copytakers on *The Independent* who get things wrong. *The Times* once printed a report filed to copytakers which was intended to suggest that Rush and Hughes would lead the Wales attack, but instead announced to the world that the Wales attack would be led by Russian Jews.

W

GRAHAM WALKER

Lead singer with the Grumbleweeds, long-running stars of BBC radio. The group, Robin Colvill, Maurice Lee and Graham Walker, have been together since 1962.

A policeman was interviewing a chap about his wife's death.

'What happened?' he asked.

'Well, I didn't realise my wife was at the red tee getting ready to swing. I drove off, and the ball hit her on the head.'

'Yes,' said the policeman, 'the coroner's report confirms that. But why was there also a golf ball up her arse?'

'Well,' said the husband. 'That was my provisional.'

JOHN WARNETT

◄○►

*BBC Radio Kent news presenter, as well as
the voice of Kent cricket. Also once upon a time a
member of a band called Zaine Griff, who had
two minor chart hits in 1980.*

Bob 'The Cat' Bevan and I were playing in a Kent beneficiary game at Dartford.

The Cat was brought on to bowl his usual filth, and sent up another looping off-break, slower than a very slow thing going slowly. On the second bounce it hit the hapless batsman on the pad as he propped forward, and Cat turned to the umpire and bellowed an appeal in true Richard Ellison style.

'Not out!' said the umpire in a booming, confident tone.

Cat incandescently stared at said umpire and said, 'And why, oh mystic one in white, would that not be out? Did the ball not hit the batsman on the pad, smack in front of middle stump?'

'Indeed it did, Mr Cat,' said the umpire.

'So it's out then,' replied Cat.

'No, sir – it wouldn't have reached!'

STEVE WATKIN

◄○►

*Glamorgan and England opening bowler
who took over 900 wickets in a career stretching
from 1986 to 2001. In his three Tests,
he took eleven wickets.*

We were in Liverpool playing Lancashire in a four-day game and one of the players organised a team meal. He was really excited and informed us that he had found a lovely place to eat, a restaurant called the 'Merci Vous' – a nice French restaurant we thought. The player had organised the taxis and we were to be in the reception at 7 p.m. We all jumped into the taxis and travelled for about 10 minutes to the address given, where the taxi driver dropped us off.

There were a few restaurants in the vicinity but we walked up and down for about twenty minutes trying to find the French restaurant. Our patience ran out so we decided to ask in one of the establishments – a Beefeater – where the 'Merci Vous' was.

The lady replied, 'I haven't heard of any restaurant around here by that name but we do have a lovely Mersey view!'

The player suddenly realised that the receptionist had informed him the place she had booked for us was a Beefeater with a Mersey view – the Glamorgan player shall remain nameless! (It wasn't me!)

VINCE WELLS

━━━━━━━━━━◄○►━━━━━━━━━━

*Kent, Leicestershire and Durham all-rounder,
who made nine Limited Overs International
appearances for England.*

During my time as captain at Leicestershire, our great fast bowler Devon Malcolm complained of double vision and dizziness. Eventually we persuaded him to go off to see the physio.

He returned with a great big smile, to inform me that his contact lens had split in half!

What a great guy!

MIKE WESTON

<o>

England fly-half or centre who played 29 internationals in the 1960s, making him then England's most capped three-quarter. He captained the team five times, and toured twice with the British Lions.

My first meeting with Bill McLaren

Before the Scotland v England game at Murrayfield in March 1968, the England team stayed at the Peebles Hydro Hotel, and on the Friday morning held a practice at Peebles

Rugby Club. This practice (run by the players – no coaches in those days) was watched by hundreds of people.

Another practice was arranged in the afternoon in secret, to organise a 'short line-out' ploy to try to nullify Peter Stagg, the giant Scottish forward. All went well and it seemed nobody was watching, until somebody was spotted, hiding among some trees, watching us through binoculars.

Three of us ran over to him.

'My name is Bill McLaren,' he said, 'and I'm commentating on your match tomorrow. I'm just watching so that I can identify you more easily.' He then gave us a Hawick Mint Ball each, and promised he wasn't spying!

In the game itself, we were losing 6–0 into the second half. The move we had been practising was called, and Mick Coulman crashed over to score a try. Eventually we won 8–6.

After the game, Coulman and I, as captain, were interviewed by David Coleman. As we went into the BBC cabin, David said, 'I think you've already met our match commentator.'

Bill smiled and said, 'See, I didn't tell, and the move worked a treat!'

RICHARD WHITELEY

◄○►

*Countdown host, purveyor of terrible puns
and wearer of startling jackets and ties.*

During the Scarborough Festival an avid young Yorkshire fan comes upon a stall at the local fairground announcing 'Marvo, the Miracle Memory Man'.

Intrigued, the fan enters the tent and finds, to his surprise, an American Indian lounging in a chair and drawing very slowly on his pipe.

'All right mate?' says the Yorkshireman. The Indian removes the pipe from his mouth and with steely eyes says quietly, 'Where I come from, it is customary to greet a stranger with the word "How".'

Feeling a little intimidated, the fan responds, 'How, Marvo, what is this all about then?'

'I have a perfect and infallible memory' says Marvo. 'Ask me anything.'

'I'll get this bugger' says the fan to himself and asks, 'Who won the Gillette Cup Final in 1965?'

'Yorkshire beat Surrey by 175 runs, 4 September 1965.'

'That's amazing,' says the Yorkshireman, and leaves shortly afterwards.

Some 15 years later, the now-seasoned fan is back at the Festival and is most surprised to come upon Marvo the Native American Memory Man again.

'How,' he greets him.

Replies Marvo, 'Boycott 146, Illingworth 5 for 29.'

JUNE WHITFIELD

————————◄○►————————

Much-loved comedy actress whose credits range from Take It From Here *with Jimmy Edwards on the BBC Light Programme, to* Absolutely Fabulous *via* Terry and June *and* The News Huddlines.

Sir Ronald Gould, former general secretary of the National Union of Teachers and a cricket enthusiast, had three trays on his desk, which he labelled 'In', 'Out' and 'LBW'. A visitor asked the meaning of LBW, and the cricket enthusiast replied, 'Let the b******s wait'.

JPR WILLIAMS

A Welsh rugby legend, one of the greatest full backs of all time, who also won Junior Wimbledon in 1966! Capped 55 times for his country between 1969 and 1981, then a record, he was also part of two Lions tours. After retirement from rugby, he became an orthopaedic surgeon.

Bobby Windsor, the hooker of the famous Pontypool front row, was on tour to South Africa in 1974. He decided to order an omelette for his lunch.

The waiter asked him, 'Do you want mushroom, cheese or ham?'

Bobby replied, 'Egg omelette, please.'

SHAUN WILLIAMSON

For many years he was Barry in EastEnders *until his untimely tumble off a cliff early in 2004. Subsequently seen as a quiz-show host, as well as being a brilliant cabaret entertainer.*

Jimmy Greaves recounts how Bill Shankly was once accused of taking his wife to watch Accrington Stanley play on their wedding anniversary.

'That story is wrong on two counts,' he said. 'For a start it was Accrington Stanley Reserves, and it wasn't our anniversary, it was my wife's birthday. As if I would have got married in the football season!'

JULIAN WILSON

—◄○►—

*Well-known racing journalist, keen Lord's Taverner
and slow left-arm bowler of much guile.*

Every spring the Earl and Countess of March invite
an assortment of guests, of varying levels of distinction, to
lunch with them at the Goodwood May Meeting. It is a
coveted invitation to England's loveliest racecourse,
where the cuisine is excellent and the horse-racing of the
highest quality.

A couple of years ago I had the good fortune to be seated
next to my attractive hostess. Her conversation was warm
and enchanting, and among other confidences, she revealed
that she enjoyed allowing her children into the family bedroom.

At this point I should explain that I have a difficult rela-
tionship with most children, who are quite reasonably terri-
fied of me (and vice versa), and whom I describe as 'goblins'.

Some weeks after my lunch with the Marchs, my friend
Rory Bremner telephoned and mentioned that he had been
invited to lunch with the family at Glorious Goodwood in
July.

'What are they like?' asked Rory.

'They're fine,' I replied. 'Very hospitable. The only thing
about Janet is that she enjoys having goblins in her bedroom.'

At the time, I was convinced that Rory was acquainted
with my unconventional terminology ...

Goodwood came and went, and Rory and I met at a Lord's
Taverners cricket match.

'How did your lunch at Goodwood go?' I asked.

'Well, all right,' replied Rory, 'until I asked Janet why she had garden gnomes in her bedroom. She didn't talk to me much after that ...'

For some reason my invitations to lunch at Goodwood have been discontinued.

REVD ANDREW WINGFIELD DIGBY

———◄○►———

Won three Blues for Oxford v Cambridge in the
1970s as a medium-pace bowler who batted a bit, and
subsequently became spiritual adviser to the England
team two decades later. A leading member of Christians
In Sport, and later vicar of St Andrew's, Oxford.

I was playing for Dorset v Devon at Dorchester. Behind the bowler's arm at the town end is a cemetery. Twice in one innings, of 12 in 3 balls, I hit the ball into the graveyard for six – it was an irresponsible knock! Next morning, the *Dorset Echo* headlined the back page, 'Rev raises the dead'.

When I arrived in the England dressing room in 1991, to be introduced as their spiritual adviser, Ian Botham spoke first. 'Don't you worry,' he said. 'Lambie and I will sing in the choir.'

Philip Tufnell, he of the Jungle, introduced me at a reception in Sydney as 'my personal spiritual adviser'. Whenever I reflect that I might be successful at anything, I remember this introduction!

GREG WISE

———◄○►———

British television and film actor, whose credits
include Johnny English *with Rowan Atkinson, and*
television adaptations of Sense And Sensibility,
The Moonstone *and* Madame Bovary.

Here's a story from my mate, the actor Jim Carter, about the cricket team I play for. Before my time, though, this one ...

34

The Royal National Theatre cricket team versus the Shoemaker's Arms, Pentrebach, South Wales, in the early 1980s.

Michael Bogdanov, a director at the National Theatre, was, bizarrely, also the landlord of the pub in the small farming village of Pentrebach (pop. very few). He invited the National team down for a Sunday match.

We turn up in our whites; the village turn up in whatever Welsh sheep-shearers and farmers call summer-wear: brown tweed and corduroy mainly. We were all still drunk or deeply hung-over from the previous night in the pub. The pitch was a damp field, bordering the river, with a roughly rolled strip in its middle. It had never hosted a cricket match before.

After first explaining the Laws to the opposition, we batted. Our straight-bat defence obviously bored the opposition to the extent that a shout went up, 'Hey boys – I've got a trout!'

Square leg, having found more interest in the river, had successfully tickled a trout. Game suspended for half an hour while we all try.

On resumption, mid-wicket, attired in brown trousers, moth-eaten sweater and tweed jacket, fell fast asleep. He caught our best batsman. The ball lodged in the jacket of his prone form. As the ball had not touched the ground, the umpire signalled 'out'. The only shame was that the fielder didn't awake from his drunken slumber to share in the rejoicing of his team-mates.

We compiled a score of about 80 in 30 overs. They knocked them off with 20 overs to spare.

The fixture, sadly, was never replayed.

JOHN WOODCOCK

The doyen of cricket writers at the turn of the century,
former cricket correspondent of The Times *and former*
editor of Wisden Cricketers' Almanack, *he has*
reported cricket from all around the world several times.

Rockley Wilson was for many years a master at Winchester, renowned for his epigrams. A leg-break bowler himself, he played many times for Yorkshire and went with the MCC side to Australia in 1920/21, playing in the last Test match.

When on his way to take the First-XI nets at Winchester at the start of a summer term, he passed the junior nets where there was a little boy in his first year at the school, being watched by his proud father.

'That's my boy there,' said the parent proudly, 'bowling left arm over the wicket. Rather like Voce, don't you think?'

'A little sotto Voce,' came the reply. 'A little sotto Voce.'

IAN WOOLDRIDGE

One of the very best of our sports journalists,
Ian Wooldridge OBE has established a reputation for
outspoken comment on many key sports issues,
over more than 40 years.

In 1963, when I was cricket correspondent of the *Daily Mail*, I had the temerity, along with luminaries like Richie Benaud and Ted Dexter, to suggest in print that Charlie Griffith, the West Indian fast bowler, illegally threw the occasional delivery.

A fat lot of good that did me two winters later when I went on a friendly cricket tour to Barbados with an English press team. They have long memories in the Caribbean.

There was much laughter among the local players during the lunch break. 'What number you batting, man?' 'About seven, I guess,' I replied. 'Well,' they said, 'we've got someone who's dying to meet you.'

The someone was Charlie Griffith's cousin whom they'd kept under wraps until my arrival in the middle. His first delivery whizzed past my head at about 120 mph. His second almost parted such hair as I had left. His third? Don't remind me. I was closer to the square leg umpire than the wicket when it scattered my stumps.

I've seen a few acts of abysmal cowardice during my years in sportswriting but that was a shameful two-white-feathers job.